CW00803030

Me and My MG

Me and My MG

Gordon Thorburn

To all who love proper cars.

First published in Great Britain in 2011 by
Remember When
An imprint of
Pen & Sword Books Ltd
47 Church Street
Barnsley
South Yorkshire
S70 2AS

Copyright © Gordon Thorburn 2011

ISBN 978 1 84468 116 7

The right of Gordon Thorburn to be identified as Author of this work
has been asserted by him in accordance with the Copyright, Designs
and Patents Act 1988.

A CIP catalogue record for this book is
available from the British Library.

All rights reserved. No part of this book may be reproduced or transmitted in
any form or by any means, electronic or mechanical including photocopying,
recording or by any information storage and retrieval system, without permission
from the Publisher in writing.

Typeset in 10pt Palatino by Mac Style, Beverley, East Yorkshire
Printed and bound by Printworks International

Pen & Sword Books Ltd incorporates the imprints of Pen & Sword Aviation,
Pen & Sword Maritime, Pen & Sword Military, Wharncliffe Local History, Pen &
Sword Select, Pen & Sword Military Classics, Leo Cooper, Seaforth Publishing and
Frontline Publishing.

For a complete list of Pen & Sword titles please contact
PEN & SWORD BOOKS LIMITED
47 Church Street, Barnsley, South Yorkshire, S70 2AS, England
E-mail: enquiries@pen-and-sword.co.uk
Website: www.pen-and-sword.co.uk

Contents

Pete and Fran Thelander of Westminster, California, just had time for a *quattro stagione* pit-stop before the race at Laguna Seca, Monterey. Here is Pete overtaking a 1960s H Modified car of uncertain origin, in his 1934 MG NE, one of only seven ever built as a racing variant of the N-type Magnette.

I've told you, you are not getting in this car until I say so.

Xavier Boucheron and his TB, registered in Lancashire, 1939, here in modern-day Montmartre. It's the Rue du Mont-Cenis to be exact, painted by Maurice Utrillo not long before the TB was built, and the old MG looks right at home.

Author's Note

Proper cars have leather seats, veneered dashboards, circular instrument dials with chrome rims, black knobs with 'CHOKE' engraved in white, large steering wheels (preferably wood and metal), wipers and heaters that don't work very well, and a hole in the front for a starting handle. They have cigar lighters, ashtrays and possibly fold-down Bakelite trays in the back. They require more of the driver than that he or she simply sit there, one finger on the wheel. If such cars are fitted with wireless telegraph receivers, they will have knobs that you turn rather than multi-function buttons that never do what you expect or want.

Such a perception of the motor car is of course born of the cars of my youth. My father's first car was a Ford Popular circa 1954, HUB 441, brown, although we had toured Scotland before that in a huge, borrowed pre-war car, something like a Morris Oxford 16 I should say. Other people had Humber Super Snipes, MG TCs, Mark VIII Jags, and so on. My second experience of 100mph was in a Mark VIII, that my friend Jim bought in 1968 for £17.10s.0d. That was on the Kingston bypass, and six weeks later the big ends went on the A1 near Doncaster. My first ton, since you ask, was as a passenger in a Morgan Plus Four on the Leeds ring road in about 1966.

After many years of being denied such experiences, I thought it would be a good idea to do a book on the people who still have such cars, and much older ones, and who understand and love them and rebuild them as necessary. The best starting point seemed to be the most popular make, and there is no doubt that of all the cars in all the world, the one with the greatest number of enthusiasts, clubs, events and so on, is the MG.

You will note I used the word 'people'. In fact, they all turned out to be men. No women responded to my pleas. Women are in the book, women who enjoy the cars but as wives and girlfriends, not as principals in the deal. Explanations of this men-only phenomenon should be written on one side of a postage stamp and sent to Boys with Toys Limited, Abingdon, Berkshire. And there's nothing wrong with that, is there, boys?

Introduction

Immense, breath-snatching, passionate

'Glancing back they saw a small cloud of dust, with a dark centre of energy, advancing on them at incredible speed, while from out the dust a faint 'Poop-poop!' wailed like an uneasy animal in pain. Hardly regarding it, they turned to resume their conversation, when in an instant (as it seemed) the peaceful scene was changed, and with a blast of wind and a whirl of sound that made them jump for the nearest ditch, It was on them! The 'poop-poop' rang with a brazen shout in their ears, they had a moment's glimpse of an interior of glittering plate-glass and rich morocco, and the magnificent motor car, immense, breath-snatching, passionate, with its pilot tense and hugging his wheel, possessed all earth and air for the fraction of a second, flung an enveloping cloud of dust that blinded and enwrapped them utterly, and then dwindled to a speck in the far distance, changed back into a droning bee once more…

Toad sat straight down in the middle of the dusty road, his legs stretched out before him, and stared fixedly in the direction of the disappearing motor car. He breathed short, his face wore a placid, satisfied expression, and at intervals he faintly murmured 'Poop-poop!'

This extract is from *The Wind in the Willows* by Kenneth Grahame, published in 1908. There were no MGs then, but it might have been a Cadillac Model A (1903), or a Rolls-Royce 10hp, a Rover 5hp or possibly a Lanchester 12hp four cylinder. The point remains the same.

No, I won't. Get lost

The evil spirit appeared in a dream, saying cars are rubbish. Cars are mere machines. The dreamer, who could have been any one of the men and women in this book, was shouting 'Oh no they're not!'.

'But you must see,' said the evil spirit, 'that every sensible family should have a nice, reliable diesel five seater in the garage, with room for the dog and the shopping and the holiday suitcases. Or, if all you're doing is going to work, a clever, super-economical little electro-whizzbox is all a commuter needs. Beyond that, nothing. Nothing at all. What's the point? What's a car? Heap of tin. Goes from A to B. Cheaper by taxi anyway. Haaa-ha-ha-ha-ha-ha-ha-ha-ha-haaaa!'

The dreamer awoke in a sweat. Was it true, what the evil spirit had said? Was that really all that motoring life could offer?

Varied though they be, the dreamers in this book have something in common: a refusal to accept such defeat. The cars featured here are all MGs, and they are all unsuitable, in one way or another, for life in the modern world but their owners

will not give in. They would rather love – and sometimes despair of – a vehicle with faults in its character, than have no feelings about one that has no character at all.

That these people are besieged by great forces is apparent. Around them runs a stream of automobiles with fuel-injected air-conditioned sports warranties and four-wheel three-year ABS alloy airbags. These cars bong at you with the startling news that you have left the door open, the handbrake is on, you haven't fastened your belt yet, it's cold outside and you've switched the satnav woman off.

Such vehicles are gigahertzably complex inside, entirely reliant on technology which cannot be seen or touched, and their outsides cannot be told one from another. They are, in fact, computerised heaps of tin, eminently suitable for going from A to B, but only for that, and they are no fun at all.

Twisting your sinews

Such cars do not inspire the poet in his breast. They can be discussed of course, and possibly the correct one might be purchased for use but, deep down, we know that today's production cars are boring, boring, boring, like sushi, train spotting and pond linings. Riding along in one's automobile has become an experience devoid of spiritual interest.

Elegant lines; steady road-holding; a top speed of 107.6 mph; 0–60 in 11.6 seconds;* and the sort of luggage space you need when you just want to get up and go – that's the MGB GT.

A worthy stable companion to cars like the Midget, MGB and MGB GT V8.

Look out, too, for the 'limited edition' of 750 specially equipped MGB GTs, built to commemorate MG's fiftieth year.

When you're behind the wheel of an MG, you're driving a true thoroughbred.

*Source: Motor

You can do it in an MG.

Say no more.

William Blake assembled these words in his poem *The Tyger*:

'And what shoulder, and what art,
Could twist the sinews of thy heart?

Well, we have to doubt whether looking in a car showroom window today is going to do much for your heartbeat.

Love's not Time's fool though rosy lips and cheeks
Within his bending sickle's compass come;
Love alters not with his brief hours and weeks,
But bears it out, even to the edge of doom.

....as William Shakespeare put it. And we are at the edge of doom. This is what we are come to. Unless we love, and alter not, it will soon be all over. Farewell MG. Hello Korean people-carrier.

From Genghis Khan to Daewoo Musso

Genghis Khan may have fired the first internal combustion engine, or cannon, in about 1200. Brother Berthold Schwartz, a monk, did fire his in Freiburg, now in Germany, then an independent city, around 1313. Anyway, neither knew that, by their efforts, an inexorable process had thus begun which would culminate in, among other things, this book.

Of course, the cannon as the prototype of the IC engine had a number of obvious drawbacks. You could rarely retrieve the piston to use again, the fuel was a bit iffy and revs per minute were poor.

Another man of the cloth, the Abbé Hautefeuille of Orleans, proposed some answers in 1678 in his design for a joined-up powder engine, and Christiaan Huygens, noted physicist, actually built such a thing. His valves were made of leather and didn't work very well so, by about 1690, most scientific folk agreed that gunpowder was not really the energy source with which to move forward.

Leonardo da Vinci had made drawings for a clockwork car in the 1470s but nobody saw that leading eventually to the MGB GT V8, the Armstrong Siddeley Sapphire or, for that matter, the Scammel six ton mechanical horse with tipping trailer. More helpful was his crankshaft, perfectly described if hand driven, but not known to Monsieur Nicolas Joseph Cugnot 300 years later, who used a click-bonk-clunk arrangement of pawls and cogwheels to convert reciprocating linear into step-by-step rotary action in his *Fardier à vapeur* (steam dray).

Jerking along at two miles an hour, this massive three-wheeled cart had to stop every three hundred yards to work up steam again. It probably caused the first case of travel sickness and certainly featured in the first automobile crash when it ran through a wall. Monsieur Cugnot, pioneer so many times over, had his pension stopped and was exiled by Napoleon, and so died in poverty.

'I wanted a new frock, not a spit!'

There were inventors all over Europe and America working at something, they knew not what, but it had to be a motive force better than steam. In England, John Barber

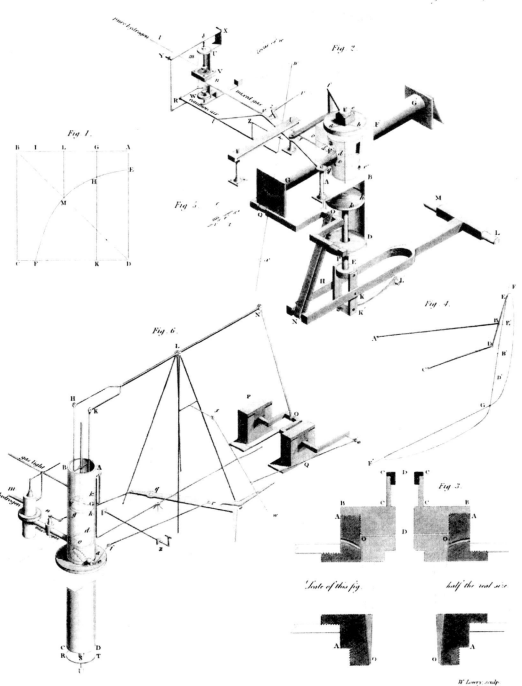

The Reverend Cecil's hydrogen engine, 1820, was meant to be convenient, economical, versatile and easy to start, so that uniform operations might be performed with advantage.

The world's first road traffic accident involving a self-propelled vehicle occurred around 1770, when Nicolas Cugnot's steam dray, built with military use in mind, refused instructions and ran into a wall.

That's no way to treat an old lady. Pete Thelander gives his NE the gun, up and away past the rhododendrons. Other MGs wait in an orderly queue behind the marshal, their drivers hoping to perform a uniform operation with advantage.

The M.G. Car Co. Ltd., Sales Division, Longbridge, Birmingham.
Overseas Business: Nuffield Exports Ltd,. Cowley, Oxford & Piccadilly, W.1
12 Months' Warranty and backed by B.M.C. Service—the most comprehensive in Europe.

First of the line

FC 7900

Patriarch of a noble race—the first sports M.G. ever made—the start
of this great line of high-performance cars.
40 years its junior is M.G.'s latest model, the M.G.B.
Styles have changed but the excitement of those early sports cars
is still there, because M.G.s are still made by
M.G. enthusiasts with enthusiasts like you in mind.
Try the superlative M.G.B. for real 'Safety Fast' motoring.

Safety Fast **MGB** *£690 plus £144.6.3 P.T.*
(whitewall tyres and overdrive optional extra)

developed a kind of dragon's breath engine that blew ignited gas against a small waterwheel style turbine. An American, Samuel Morey, began with a steam-driven spit to help his wife in the kitchen but, in 1823, 'having accidentally discovered' that a mixture of steam, gaseous spirits of turpentine and air became highly explosive, he declared that he had 'given the mechanical world a new power'. We can only wonder how his accidental discovery came about and, alas, poor old Morey was already twenty years behind the times.

Robert Street in England had built an engine in 1794 with a cylinder and piston, driven by turpentine vapour. A fire outside the cylinder evaporated the turpentine and another flame lit it, and bang. Philippe Lebon described a more sophisticated version working on coal gas in 1801 and may even have built a working version, had he not died from an ultra-mugging in Paris in 1804.

Of a dozen more working on the same idea, the Swiss François de Rivaz made an engine running on a hydrogen/oxygen mixture in 1807 but he found it hard to persuade people to stand near it. His design for a horseless carriage, using the same engine and fuel, attracted a similar level of enthusiasm.

To produce a moving Power in Machinery

The Reverend W Cecil MA of Papworth Everard, Fellow of Magdalen College and of the Cambridge Philosophical Society, read a paper to the said Society, 27 November 1820. His starting point was: 'There is scarcely any uniform operation in the Arts which might not be performed with advantage by machinery, if convenient and economical methods could be found for setting such machinery in motion'. He gave himself additional criteria: that the Power should be easy and quick to start, and be able to operate anywhere. His hydrogen engine (an elegant operation in the Arts indeed, see diagram) filled the bill. It worked, at 60rpm, but was never a practical proposition for setting really useful machinery in motion.

Mr Samuel Brown was not at the varsity. He took the Reverend Cecil's principles and produced a 'gas-vacuum' engined vehicle in 1826, belted up Shooter's Hill in it, then built and sold some engines which performed regular service in, for example, Croydon.

Other gas engines were proposed and built but it was Jean Lenoir, a famous Belgian, who produced a spark-ignition version which worked at commercial speeds and was reasonably reliable in some circumstances. He put it in a carriage in 1860 but the racket was unbearable and the engine kept seizing. Most of the five hundred engines he sold drove static machinery.

Ardent spirits

The Reverend Cecil said you could use coal gas, turpentine or vapour of oil (petrol/gasoline vapour) instead of hydrogen, 'or any ardent spirit: but none of these have been tried' by him, because he didn't think they'd be as good. Well, he was wrong.

Until the mid 1880s, the lighter slices of oil were regarded as too dangerous. Town-gas engines were heavy and slow, yes, but petrol...hmm, what about lamp oil? While Yorkshire lad Bill Priestman was building his lamp-oil engine, Herr Gottlieb Daimler developed his light, fast, reliable, small, powerful motor which used the established Otto four-stroke cycle and which ran on...vapour of oil.

Daimler didn't like putting his motor in road vehicles, though. He preferred boats. Karl Benz preferred tricycles, and he had quite a good little engine running on benzine (no relation), also called ligroin, being that petroleum fraction consisting mainly of C7 and C8 hydrocarbons. So Daimler met Benz, Krebs met Panhard, De Dion met Bouton, everyone decided on four wheelers and a less refined fraction, C5 to C12, called petrol, or gasoline, or *essence, benzin, benzina* or **бензин**, and that's how we got the Ford Edsel, the FSO, the Datsun Bluebird and the MG.

So, we have the MG. Do we want it?

Maybe you can drive my car

The single biggest difference between driving a modern car and what we might call a proper car, is that in the modern car they have removed almost everything about driving. All the carry-on that makes the car go has been insulated, silenced and placed out of reach, and the governance thereof has been given over to computerised controls. Even the basic functions of driving – steering, accelerating, braking – are not entirely the driver's, and changing gear need not be the driver's at all.

Doubtless this is all very good for road safety. It allows boy racers to concentrate utterly on rounding corners at maximum speed while not having to worry about advancing the ignition, whether they've left the choke out, or double declutching because the syncromesh has packed up. The same benefits apply to the great majority of car users, who do not want to know anything about the car's innards. Driving in today's traffic is difficult enough without all that prehistoric nonsense.

You could argue that the time and money spent in designing, making and fitting rain-activated windscreen wipers was, indeed, productive time and money and an appropriate development for the 21st century. Or, you could say I'd rather activate my own wipers and, for that matter, have other connections to my actual driving.

Not everyone wants to go the whole hog, of course. Not everyone wants a crash gearbox. Not everyone wants steering and brakes that demand almost as much planning and clairvoyance as driving a narrowboat on a canal. Some people prefer a heater to overcoat, muffler, sheepskin mittens and fur hat. Some prefer not to have to monitor constantly pressures, revolutions, temperatures, mixtures. Most certainly, they don't want to sprain their wrists and fracture their kneecaps with a starting handle.

It's the same with food. These days you don't need to know how to grow, find or catch anything to eat. You don't even need to know what food looks like in its raw state, nor do you need to know how to prepare and cook anything. If you want, you can feed yourself entirely on food with which you need not interfere in the slightest, just as you have absolutely no requirement to know what is an overhead valve Hotchkiss 1.5-litre four-cylinder engine giving about 38bhp, or a Hartford friction damper.

Unless, of course, you want to drive an MG.

This astonishing restoration, of a very rare car by David Card, is everything under the sun about old cars, all in one. When David saw the wreck in the bushes, he could also see the car as she used to be. Most people would see a heap of old iron fit only for the nearest gypsy scrap collector. David saw a 1926 bullnose MG Super Sports, a machine of extraordinary beauty in blue. He was so excited by that image, and by the thought of giving life to an animal on the verge of extinction, that he was prepared to make the commitment, even though he understood exactly what that would mean.

A new 1926 car with a new 1926 engine, ex works, price…well, you can't worry too much about that when you've put your heart and soul into it.

CHAPTER ONE

The Time Machine

David Card who lives near Reading, Berkshire, has been involved with MG rebuilds and restorations since 1971. Such knowledge and background equipped him to envisage the possibilities of a wreck, seen through a curtain of nettles and ivy, on Good Friday 1990. He already knew something about the 'simple joy' – as he calls it – of bringing an old car back from the dead, but here, in front of him, sitting in its very own wildlife garden, was the challenge of all challenges.

About three hundred and forty of the 14/28 bullnose were made, between 1924 and 1926, starting as a modified Morris Oxford with aluminium two-tone body work. Described by Cecil Kimber as 'our popular MG saloon', the model was really the MG marque in transition, the link between Morris and MG as separate entities and, with only ten surviving in the world, almost the missing link.

Responsibility for one-tenth of the entire species lies with David Card:

'The first thing to do when contemplating the restoration of any vintage car is to learn as much as possible about the vehicle. This will lead you up many fascinating highways and byways and not a few garden paths, but you will graduate to being able to identify just what work is going to be needed and what parts must be discovered or made. This can be an especially rewarding journey if, as I was, you are dealing with a rare car about which little authoritative information exists.

'One of the great things about early cars is that every assembly can be disassembled, every part can be seen, touched, felt, measured, described and made, every component can be repaired and joined with its brothers. In other words, early cars are unsophisticated. This not to say they are simple or crude, but they are mechanical, not electronic. The corollary of all that is that you can do most of the work yourself, if you are reasonably confident and competent in mechanics and willing to learn, and you can do it in your own garage with ordinary tools.

'The key to keeping going is to attack it bit by bit. Take each element as a task in itself, to be completed for its own worth, and you will be surprised how satisfying it is when the bits start coming together. When the chassis is complete and on four wheels, you can start to see the car and gain extra inspiration for the long road to completion.

'When the job is finished and you're on the open road, you will soon forget the long, long hours of oily toil in a cold garage. You will know only that unique pleasure and delight to be had from being able to say "Look at this. Isn't it amazing? And I did it." And it is amazing, too, as you can easily prove by driving down any street and watching the reactions of passers-by.

'Comparisons can be made with other kinds of restoration – pictures, furniture, books and so on. The difference with old cars is that you can get in them and go somewhere, experiencing what the original driver did all those years ago. Everything about driving a vintage car is different to the modern equivalent – the handling, the smell, the vibration, the sound, and the amount of skill and effort you have to put to it. Modern cars require very little input from the driver and, likely enough, will soon require none at all apart from being told the destination.

'With vintage cars you're going back in time, to when driving was driving, and it's your machine you're driving, you're very own time machine.'

That's a most inspiring message, David. In the interests of balance, we ought also to mention the other sort of time, the time that it took you to do the restoration – thousands of hours over nine years. During those years, the Cards moved house three times, and David kept several other difficult cars on the road. MG should give him a medal.

Much missed in the MG world is the great French racer Jacques Potherat, seen here driving his PA. The racer below is a 1936 TA Special.

This page and opposite: Richard Hartington's Maggie, in a state of undress and in full flow.

CHAPTER TWO

My Heart Belongs to Maggie

A chap called Richard Huntington decided he wanted an exciting old car. No, he needed an exciting old car. His wife Valerie, also something of a petrol head having come from a car-dealing, forecourt-owning family, concurred and so they began their search. At last, lines began to converge to a point and at that point was the marque MG – but, should it be the type favoured by 1940s and 50s RAF officers, the TC? No, too *outré*. The B was discarded as too common, the C as too dangerous, and so Madame – for it was she – took her man along to see, for the first time in his life, an MGA.

He was smitten. Never had he been so overwhelmed, so engulfed by beauty since sighing, those years ago, over Catherine Deneuve. Alas, this particular MGA was a rust bucket and painted in Caramac Orange. It would not do at all. Now that a fellow was in love, something nearer to perfection was required.

An expert was commissioned to begin with an original chassis and gradually build the dream, at a price of £14,000 which was a lot of money in 1986.

Over the weeks and months our chap, madame, and their offspring, went often to the workshop to see their car being born. They gave it a name, 'Maggie', and speculated on the wondrousness of travelling in it. How they would spin along the country lanes around Leamington Spa. How they would zip along the B4455, as the Fosse Way is now so depressingly known, perhaps to picnic by the lake at Compton Verney, or to pop in to the Heritage Motor Centre, there to chortle over the world's largest collection of old British cars not having an MGA in it.

As the thousands of quids were pressed in stages into a Swarfega'd hand, the looked-for development of components into car was not consequent. The MGA was not happening. An amount of £12,000 was reached with no bodywork attached. Our man questioned the builder on the likelihood of his completing the car within the space of the last £2,000. Such a thing was, he agreed, not written in the Book of Heavenly and Earthly Possibilities.

There were options. The builder would buy back the incomplete vehicle for the same £12,000 or, should another £4,500 be forthcoming, the car would be finished, no question. Satisfaction guaranteed, even if it ran over budget.

Some many weeks later, a beaming, joyous man sat in a red leather seat in a sparkling, as-new MGA painted in Old English White. There was bliss all around. Not long after, he was made redundant. Money was short. The children were living off soup made from the butcher's apron. Everything was sold, except Maggie.

Came the new job and the new house in south east Devon. And so, each sunny Sunday, Maggie is brought out and given a shortish trip, to Lyme Regis maybe, or Topsham, which trips in real terms cost more per mile than a moon landing, and our chap beams as before, and sighs, and looks forward to his retirement when, perhaps, he might make love with Maggie more often.

CHAPTER THREE

'Side Windows are Complete and Included'

Another quotation from the eBay description was 'As with any 60 year old car, there is no warranty'. Possibly Bob Stein, of Norfolk, Virginia, should have taken more notice of that sentence; possibly not.

Bob's doom had been sealed around the age of seven, when he read a book by Don Stanford called *The Red Car*. In this classic and entirely realistic tale, the boy hero befriends a retired Bugatti mechanic called Frenchie, and together they restore a wreck of a TC and win the local road race.

Many years later, having got no further with his destiny than a poster on the bedroom wall, Bob bought a British Coach Works replica TD, fibreglass, VW chassis, 1981 version of a 1952 car, but a very good lookalike. The drawback was poor performance, 70mph tops, which was improved with a new 1600 engine, and many admiring glances ensued at shows, from people who thought her the real thing.

Still, there was something. Bob was very fond of his replica but a little itch remained to be scratched, even by a man who now admits to having owned around 130 different vehicles since he was 16, from a 1929 Ford pickup to a 1962 Centaur folding scooter to a 1970 Lincoln and several that were halfway sensible, although whether that description fitted his TR7 we cannot say.

A mysteriously prescient friend led Bob to a website, and a TC for sale, and he was going to buy it, but a twitch of the finger of fate took him to eBay and, with four seconds to go, he made the winning bid of $25,166 for Wildflower, a 1949 TC, allegedly well maintained after restoration, 35,000 miles on the clock, and Bob's heart's desire. The car he'd wanted since dreaming in class at Fairlawn Elementary, was his. And how did he celebrate? Champagne cocktails? Dinner at the best restaurant in town? Tickets for the show? Retrieve ancient copy of *The Red Car* from cardboard box and re-read it? You choose.

TC5308 arrived from Florida at 7am, a week late, but beautiful and in good shape. A new battery powered up most of the electrics, the wipers and the fuel pump worked, the carburettors were not properly fitted and they were not a matching pair but that was no problem. A pile of spares that came with the car contained the right bits. By the evening of Day Three, she was ready to go.

Bob cranked her up and heard 'a loud clack'. Taking off the valve cover he found a broken rocker arm shaft. Disappointing, yes, but no reason to fall out of love. These things are sent to try us. While sorting out what needed to be done, Bob could still look at her, the fulfilment of a lifetime's yearning, and he could fit a new Brooklands steering wheel even though she wasn't going anywhere yet, and he could sit in the driver's seat and go 'Vroom, vroom' (no, he didn't do that last bit).

Other matters such as fuel lines, spark plugs and points were attended to, the valve train was reassembled, and the moment had come. We can do no better than quote Bob's own words:

'I took a deep breath and pulled the starter knob. She sputtered a little, and it took a few tries, but she finally caught on her own and smoothed out with no smoke, no leaks, and 50 pounds of oil pressure at warm idle. She has a miss that is probably due to maladjusted valves, which I will take care of tonight. I haven't taken her out of the garage yet, but the clutch felt smooth and the transmission snicked nicely into all gears – the brakes held when I let the clutch out. All I need now are brake lights. WOO-HOO!!!'

That seems to sum it up, really. After three further months' work, with more than a little help from his friends, replacing or remaking or repainting dozens of major and minor items that were incorrect in some way, Bob won senior first prize at the Gettysburg show of the Antique Automobile Club of America.

For the full story, see www.caroholic.com.

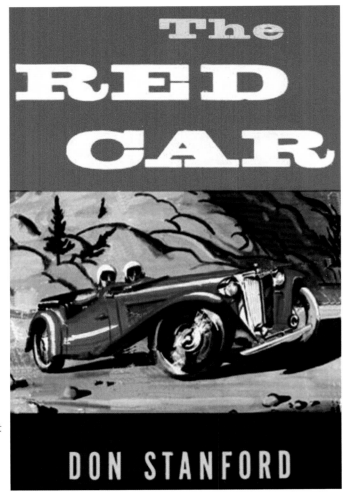

If you think you might want a T series MG but you're not entirely sure, you need to read *The Red Car* by Don Stanford.

CHAPTER FOUR

And Is There Honey Still For Tea?

The late, great Scottish comedian Chick Murray was taking tea one afternoon in a smart cafe. The waitress brought toast with one of those tiny individual pots of honey. 'Ah,' said Chick. 'I see you keep a bee.'

This episode was almost repeated years later when Paul Hunt was looking for a dashboard emblem. At the NEC Classic Car show, Birmingham, he saw just the thing, an enamel badge with a honey bee, so he bought it. 'Do you like bees, then?' asked the stallholder. 'Yes,' said Paul. 'I've got one.' 'One?' said the stallholder. 'How do you mean, one?'

After many years of 'interesting' family cars – including a Princess 2200 and a Reliant Scimitar – readers may find it interesting that Paul should designate a Scimitar as a family car; he and his very agreeable wife Jen decided to fulfil that familiar ambition and get themselves an MG. The two kids had grown up, so……

Paul Hunt's beautiful B is about to take part in the 2010 Chepstow and District Rotary Club Wye Valley Run. His wife, Jenny, navigator extraordinaire, works out the route while the photographer (who could that be?) concentrates his lens on the car. Point made?

they bought a B, KWD 630L, and called her 'Bee', seventeen years old, in not-terrible condition considering she was being driven every day, was kept outside, and did a three hundred mile romantic round trip every week-end (you can do it in an MG). Paul spent six months' worth of spare time restoring, rebuilding and replacing previous incorrect restorations, including stripping down four Black Tulip resprays to the bare metal.

The romance remained, manifesting itself, for example, in Paul taking an hour and a half circular route to reach his local newsagent one sunny autumn Sunday morning, and a trip of 2,300 miles in five days, touching Land's End, John O'Groats, and the NSEW extremities of the UK mainland, Ardnamurchan, the Lizard, Lowestoft and Dunnet Head.

But wait. What's this? An MGB GT V8? As well? The logic will appear impeccable to all MG enthusiasts. Bee was for fun so, when Paul changed his work and forewent a company car, a daily hither-and-thither vehicle was required. Obviously, a V8 filled the bill perfectly.

BUILD YOUR OWN MODEL OF THE

M.G. SPORTS CAR!

Here's the ultimate in craftsmanship — a realistic replica of the famous British M.G. — finest model kit ever produced!

This Model masterpiece has more than 50 precision-fitted parts, including steerable front wheel assembly, semi-pneumatic tires and semi-elliptical rear springs — yet it requires only a screwdriver for assembly. Body is durable die-cast construction, chassis is heavy steel. Comes with gray primer coat — can be painted to your preference.

An absorbing, educational "father-and-son" project, the Model MT is a rugged, thrill-packed toy when assembled — or a handsome collectors' item for sports car owners and hobbyists.

Price   Made by the
$10 95   makers of
West, $11.75   world famous

MT SPORTS CAR KIT

DOEPKE

Model TOYS

FOR FREE CATALOG, WRITE TO:
The CHAS. WM. DOEPKE MFG. CO., INC., ROSSMOYNE 1, OHIO

CHAPTER FIVE

Charles Darwin's MG

Well, no, not Charles Darwin's. It's Carl Cederstrand's, but he has the same sort of views on gradual change to the original over the years. The species in this case is a TD, which Carl bought in 1955. 'I always figured that the factory sold a semi-assembled kit and what I did to solve its many problems was my business. I simply continued its engineering development.'

In fact, it was worse than that. In 1955, it was only two years after TD production ceased. In the States were almost eighty per cent of all the 30,000 TDs ever made. It was relatively easy to buy a reasonably new, even a new-smelling, TD for $1000. So what did Carl do?

We all know that love is blind. We may also be familiar with John Keats's opinion, that 'Love in a hut, with water and a crust, Is – Love, forgive us! – cinders, ashes, dust'. In Carl's case, crust rhymed with rust and, with hindsight, he'd have been better off pushing his TD into the lake and starting over with another. What he did was order new wood from the factory and rewood the body shell.

And so began a half century and more of intimacy. The TD, in Carl's view, was a wonderful looking vehicle, with handling far superior to that of any American motor of that time. That's no longer true, of course, but Carl still has his TD.

On a winding road he could leave T-Birds standing, but oh, the seat. This was, Carl concluded, the most uncomfortable driving seat anyone was ever in. For whom it was designed he could not tell, but it certainly wasn't him. While ergonomics, 'the scientific study of the efficiency of man in his working environment' (*Shorter Oxford Dictionary*) was a term not coined until 1950, and clearly had little currency in the MG drawing office as regards car drivers, the concept of comfort must surely have permeated through the parish boundaries of Abingdon.

If it had, nobody had taken any notice, and so Carl took a few of his simple steps to solve the problem. He raised the front of the seat with wedges by two inches, removed the extensions from the brake and clutch pedals, shortened the accelerator pedal, put a block of foam in the seat back to give some dorsal support, and fitted a smaller steering wheel. Now he could drive for a day and get out of the car without a line of worn cloth across his trouser legs, and without feeling that he'd been beaten through the streets with a baseball bat.

Carl was an experimental physicist by profession, working for a company that designed and made advanced biomedical testing instruments, which was a background many would say could come in handy for an MG owner. And so it did, when he changed the final gear ratio from 5.125/1, which he saw as more suitable for pulling up tree stumps than roadwork, to 4.3/1, and revamped the wiring.

'The original Lucas wiring was a disaster. My only explanation was that Lucas could never have owned an ammeter. The stop lights and the wipers, the only items

I remember being fused, had 35 or 50 amp fuses so the wires burned through before the fuses did. You used to be able to get T-shirts with a Lucas switch pictured, to be set to off, flicker or dim.' Carl fitted a new fuse box with twelve positions.

Another thing he fitted was a roll bar in the front, initially to correct excessive lean when cornering rapidly, eventually to act as first aid. When the front springs failed from fatigue on one side, it enabled him to limp home on the remaining spring. When the rear springs failed, he installed a double leaf under the new main leaf, which reduced the probability of failure in the medium term, if not the inevitability in the long.

Like the discs between imperfect vertebrae, the rubber pads between the ends of spring leaves will migrate from their proper position. Pads made from lexan polycarbonate and aluminium bronze may flow and squeeze less.

There was a time, and possibly still is, when the TD's distributor filled up with oil from the sump. The works answer was to drill a hole in the distributor, to let the oil out so it could dribble down the engine. Carl made a neat little device that also let the oil out but returned it to the sump.

As the British motor industry was dissolving into almost nothing, attempts were made by BMC, as it then was, to rationalise their Byzantine parts numbering system. One result was piles of parts at US dealerships that nobody could identify. As the dealerships closed, Carl and two T-Series friends, who could recognise any spare part from 100 yards, collected them up at 20 cents on the dollar and now have suffcent spares to run their cars for several hundred more years.

Carl Cederstrand is in his eighties now, still loving his same MG TD after 300,000 miles, though other cars have come and gone, and lives with wife Darlene in Orange, California. For a chip off the old engine block, see son Carl's company at www.cederstrandracingengines.com.

In the belief that all knowledge is valuable for its own sake, we must furnish our readers with the story behind the naming of a town after a fruit. In 1873, an application for a post office under the town's original name, the very imaginative Richland, was refused as there was another Richland not far away. Four of the town's leading citizens proposed names: Orange, Lemon, Walnut, and Olive. They could not agree and so played a game of poker, the winner to decide. Did Mr Olive win, change his mind and call it Orange? No, he didn't.

Zen and the art of Morris Garage maintenance

This photograph of the engine of Berndt Aulin's TB (see page 153) has generated some notes, written while considering certain propositions of Carl Cederstrand, experimental physicist and MG owner, thus.

There are four reasons why mechanical parts fail. Do not look further for more and deeper reasons, because there are none. We can call the four reasons 'mechanisms' – using that sense of the word meaning mechanical actions in a system of mutually adapted parts in which motion occur – and they are: adhesion; abrasion; corrosion; fatigue.

These mechanisms apply in any such system, any machine, which is to say any instrument for transmitting force, or modifying its application, that consists of a number of parts, each with a definite function. It matters not if the system was designed to fill tea bags at a rate of many thousands an hour, or to tell the time in four directions at the top of the old church tower, or to erect a fabric dome of protection over one's head in case of a sudden shower. The mechanisms of failure remain immutable.

If the system was designed in Abingdon, Berkshire, United Kingdom, with the purpose of propelling persons from A to B in a particular fashion, an examination of a collection of failed parts from that system will reveal all the evidence required. Here we can see clearly where adhesion, abrasion and corrosion have caused failure, despite our knowing perfectly well that proper, preventive lubrication can entirely eliminate these three progenitors of disorder.

As to the fourth mechanism, fatigue, there we have a matter that is problematic in the true sense of the word, in that it illustrates what is possible but not necessarily true. If your part has failed through fatigue, very likely brought about by cyclic loading and unloading, such failure could only have been prevented by the part having been made differently, or made to operate in a different way. It's a design fault.

Such design, possibly including more resistant materials, is always a compromise between function and cost. It would be possible to design and make all MG parts so that they operated perfectly and lasted effectually for ever, but where's the fun in that?

CHAPTER SIX

What Ho, Old Bean

Major General Kenneth 'Skip' Burns, USAF (Retired), has just completed forty years of ownership of a 1939 TB. It is by no means uncommon for air force officers to prefer the MG marque, especially the T Series. Indeed, during World War Two, it was almost *de rigueur* for anyone of RAF squadron leader rank or equivalent to have a TA or TB, preferably with a black labrador to jump in the back, although one young fellow just up from the varsity, a certain Pilot Officer Leonard Cheshire, joined his squadron in 1940 driving a Bentley Speed Six. However, for an American airman in 1970, the call was not quite so expected.

This was when Lieutenant Colonel Burns was posted from the war in Vietnam to the relative tranquility of the UK, to the RAF College of Air Warfare at Manby, Lincolnshire. Skip hadn't seen an MG before but, of course, as already stated, where any significant number of air force officers are gathered together, there will be MGs. The usual seduction took place.

A few months passed and Skip was transferred, back to his old job of flying fighters, at the USAF F-111 base at RAF Upper Heyford, but in a new frame of mind. He was now an MG man. Supersonic jet aircraft were all very well, and that included the English Electric Lightning, the one the RAF called the ultimate jet sports car, but on the ground there was no such excitement.

Upper Heyford is in that fair county of Oxfordshire that also contains the Hook Norton brewery and Abingdon. One day, looking through the classifieds in the local rag for nothing in particular, Skip happened across an ad for a car ten miles away in Banbury.

The widow of its former custodian wanted rid, but this car had stood doing nothing for years and did not look promising. Even so, the impulses of an air force officer in pursuit of fun could not be denied. Skip coughed up the required sum and wondered what to do next. Pumping up the tyres seemed like a good idea, and the batteries were obviously beyond redemption so a pair of six-volts were bought from the local garage. Having already learned that gas is called petrol in the UK, Skip was able to purchase a can of that too.

Much to his delight and partial astonishment, she started up. And, she seemed more or less driveable.

With great caution, Skip nursed her back to his own garage through waves of mixed emotions. What a fantastic car. What on earth have I done? I'm going to have to take her to bits. What on earth have I done, again? And so it came to pass that Abby, for that was her name now, was dismantled to her very last nut and bolt, and rebuilt using all original parts. It took four years.

The people at Abingdon heard about it and invited Skip and Abby down, to be greeted by the entire MG workforce at the plant, the factory manager H E Cecil

Cousins, and the retired racing driver Captain George E T Eyston, who wanted to take Abby for a spin around the yard. This man Captain Eyston was a previous world land speed record holder. In the 1930s he'd driven supercharged MGs like the Magic Midget and the K3 Magnette. He'd jumped out of his Midget EX120 at 60mph, when it burst into flames after setting another record by doing 100mph for an hour (see page 70).

Skip could only hope that the Captain would be kind to Abby, and so he was, and Skip's own brief racing career at Silverstone also was happily incident free but it was time to go back to the USA. Skip drove Abby to Folkstone, for shipping to Texas, where she enjoyed her new life until Skip was posted overseas again. Abby went into storage for seventeen years.

Re-acquaintance required only petrol and batteries and air in the tyres, just like the first meeting, only this time everything worked including the clock and the 30mph warning light. In 2000, she won Best Antique Car in Texas, at the Houston show.

If you happen to be in Texas, and you happen to see a TB bowling along, you will know if it's Abby. She has a double tyre rack at the back, with a rattan basket on top. The basket has spares inside but outside, fixed to it with leather straps, is the ultimate British sporting symbol: a cricket bat.

Skip Burns's TB, complete with picnic basket and cricket bat, but where are Jeeves and Wooster?

For our kind of motoring—

it must be an M.G.

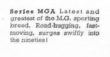

Series MGA Latest and greatest of the M.G. sporting breed. Road-hugging, fast-moving, surges swiftly into the nineties!

Series MGA Coupé Lovely, lively, fast and well-mannered. Brilliant sports motoring in all-weather luxury.

M.G. Magnette Liveliest saloon in its class. Sumptuously appointed, delightful to drive—real sports motoring in luxury!

Safety fast !

M.G. Magnette Varitone Sports saloon—plus! Wrap-round rear window, choice of eight two-tone finishes. Manumatic two-pedal control (optional extra on all Magnettes).

THE M.G. CAR COMPANY LIMITED, SALES DIVISION, COWLEY, OXFORD
London Showrooms: Stratton House, 80 Piccadilly, London, W.1
Overseas Business: Nuffield Exports Limited, Cowley, Oxford, and 41 Piccadilly, London, W.1

Twelve Months'
Warranty and
backed by
BMC Service—the most
comprehensive in Europe.

131

Motor magazine, October 1957.

CHAPTER SEVEN

Using Your Skill and Judgement

In no more than twenty-five words complete the following sentence: 'I like my Papermate pen because …'.

The man reading those words, in a newspaper in 1953, had a stepson in his first year at the Southern Methodist University, Dallas. The second prize in the Papermate pen competition, run by a Texas drug-store chain, was a year's college scholarship. That would come in very handy, thought the man, so he put his mind to the matter of why his stepson might prefer a ballpoint pen, then a relative novelty, to the more usual fountain pen. He reasoned that college students would be a major target market for Papermate, so he cobbled something together, in exactly twenty-five words, about how the pen was equally marvellous for classroom note taking, essays, examinations and letters to the folks back home, sent it in and forgot about it.

Some weeks later, a secretary interrupted a class at the university, saying that a student, Ed Reynolds, had to come to the office to take an important phone call. On the line was the owner of the drug-store chain, a Mr Skillran, who was delighted to tell Ed that he had won first prize in the Papermate pen competition.

What? No, no, that couldn't be right. Ed protested that Mr Skillran had the wrong guy, because he, Ed, had not entered that competition nor, indeed, had he entered any such competition ever in his life. Mr Skillran insisted. The name on the entry was Ed Reynolds, at this college, with this telephone number, and so he was the winner.

'OK. What have I won?' asked Ed.

'You have won a brand new sports car, an MG TD, just shipped over from England, and I want you to come to my headquarters this afternoon, to accept the keys and have your picture taken for the papers.'

The debut year of ownership went by without much trouble. Ed drove the car back and forth between college and home in Connecticut and clocked up his first 25,000 miles, then he did some engineering work on it that involved fitting a new polished aluminium valve cover and, soon after, suffered extensive damage when somebody ran into the back of him at a stop light.

The crash damage was put right, seemingly, and over the next couple of years Ed came to assume that it was normal for TDs to burn out their valves every 25,000 miles because that's what happened, without fail. He became an engine overhaul expert but, alas, did not replace a faulty gasket in quick enough time to prevent his brother taking the car for an unauthorised spin with a drastic oil leak. The damage became apparent later, on the Pennsylvania turnpike as Ed drove back to college and the engine blew. There was nothing to be done except ship her back to Connecticut and live without her for the winter.

The year of 1957 was an important one in Ed's life. He had his TD's engine rebuilt to racing spec by the mechanics at Briggs Cunningham's works, and he joined the air force. Driving was now an extra pleasure, between navigator training schools in Texas, but Ed's first posting, to Bangor, Maine, almost marked the end of his beautiful friendship. Maine winters and open-top temperamental sports cars do not fit neatly together, so Ed went to a car dealership to trade in his TD for a more sensible, enclosed car.

The dealer was not impressed by the MG and offered $100, so Ed bought the sensible car and kept the MG, a decision that proved to be right when he was transferred to Bermuda. Meanwhile, he had met Judy, his wife-to-be, in Maine and the wedding coincided with a posting to California. Judy had a Volkswagen Beetle. Neither car could tow the other so they both drove to California. The range on a full tank was about the same for both cars but the TD went up hills faster, while the VW was quicker going down them, so Ed and Judy met during their honeymoon days at gas stations and waved at each other on hills.

A posting to New Hampshire re-posed the winter problem, this time solved with a removable hard top and a window defroster, and twenty two more years passed, to 1979. In that year, the car's wiring gave up and Ed retired from the air force. Peeling back wire insulation revealed green powder, which explained why the brake lights didn't work.

Settled in a new job in California, Ed decided that a complete restoration was necessary. Some detective work led him to the ex-foreman of a former MG repair shop in San Francisco, and a deal was done on a frame-up rebuild. The job got as far as the deconstruction, but the reconstruction was stymied by the sudden disappearance of the mechanic. More detective work by a lawyer, who was also having his MG restored, identified the man as a body in the morgue, the previously unknown victim of a mugging murder.

Ed loaded up the heap of bits that had been his car and took the lot to Santa Clara, to O'Connor Classic Autos, where the magic man Mike O'Connor told him that the frame had been bent since the 1954 stop-light collision, and that this particular TD, one of the last to be made, had a TF head and so needed different valve clearance settings to the standard TD. So that, you see, was why the valves burned out so regularly.

Seeing as Ed had had the car from new, it was decided to restore it as the original rather than as an improved version. It meant – for example – finding new tyres of the correct Dunlop 5.50 x 15 size, in Zimbabwe, and a lot more expenditure while ignoring many advances made in automobile engineering in half a century. But, it was worth it, because the finished car was almost exactly as she had been in 1953, so she won lots of prizes at shows and, after all, being a prize herself, she hadn't cost Ed anything to buy.

CHAPTER EIGHT

Snowplough Partly Consumed by Horse

On 16 of July 1946, the Kent Police Authority approved a request from the Kent Constabulary for nine new patrol cars. These were to be MG TCs, each costing £496 17s 11d. Using a simple conversion via the UK retail price index, this sum translates as about fifteen thousand pounds in modern terms but that's not really the whole story. If you look at £500 in terms of earnings, when a police constable (for example) would be lucky to be on £500 a year including allowances, that figure of £15,000 more than doubles. Cars also were in short supply after the war; they had a rarity value. So, with nine TCs, Kent police were making quite an investment at a current equivalent of around fifty thousand pounds per car.

Police Constable Barnes poses in his patrol car in Margate, Kent, in the morning sun of 1947. It was customary then for police officers to wear their medal ribbons and, from the row across PC Barnes's chest, it seems that he did his bit in the last war. The car is one of the HKR range but not 473, which was assigned to the Rochester area.

All nine were delivered on the same day from Gatward's of Maidstone with successive registration numbers, HKR 471 to HKR 479. We know that HKR 473 was commissioned into service on 13 September 1946, and we know that she is still running around Nova Scotia.

In 1946, the police officers who drove the TCs in their law enforcement role were quite affectionate towards them. Perhaps today's traffic cops feel affection too, towards their super-efficient, mega-equipped vehicles; perhaps not, but then they can't lift themselves out of their seats to look over the top of the windscreen in fog.

Besides this unexpected advantage, the police issue 1946 TC had a top speed of 90mph and did about 25 miles to the gallon. We don't have 0–60 figures but officers driving them described the acceleration as 'very good', likewise the road holding. They also described how making a sharp U-turn on a cambered road could make sparks fly from the low-slung exhaust. In snow, the front number plate acted as a snowplough blade, throwing clouds of the freezing white stuff up and over the bonnet.

One officer left his car to interview a witness, only to find on his return that his soft-top had been half eaten by a horse. Another had a burn on his finger for the rest of his life, where his wedding ring had touched the pins of an inspection lamp as he plugged it into the dashboard socket. Yet another found himself to be just the right size to whack his kneecap on the door handle as he got out in a hurry.

Getting out was a necessity in winter, the custom for the cops being to run briskly up and down the road in an attempt to warm up after a sojourn in the heater-less patrol car. There was no radio either, and this was the reason for the MGs being replaced in 1948 with the Wolseley 14, which was a more substantial vehicle better able to take the weight of wireless sets and extra batteries although, as it turned out, less suited to police work. Delivery of radios was delayed and the Wolseleys were near wrecks by the time they came.

HKR 473 was sold to a dealer, Elvridge and Sons, for £430 in November 1948. So little depreciation over two years of hard use – although expert maintenance – reflects the shortage of new cars in post-war Britain. The dealer sold her to Mr Maurice Edwin Steptoe of Canterbury in January of 1949, and he sold to Mr Leslie George Andrews, also of Canterbury, in 1952. The next owner, from 1953, was Mr Bradbury Baker of Chatham, and then the trail goes cold until 1971 when a Canadian, B H Pollock, an Athlone Scholar (Canadian equivalent to Rhodes scholarships) then living in Wootton Bassett, decided he loved his MG TC HKR 473 so much that he would have to ship her back to Montreal with him.

Lovers can be fickle, even MG lovers, and Mr Pollock fell for a Bugatti, to pay for which he had to sell his TC and his two Porsche 356s. He advertised in the *Montreal Star*, and a fellow in Sydney, Nova Scotia, who had lived in Montreal, happened to pick up the paper and see the ad. This fellow, Barc Cunningham, was a civil engineer of an old Nova Scotia family going back to the 1760s there. If Barc goes back in his own time to teenage years, he can vividly recall a trip from New Brunswick, up to Sydney and back, an 800 mile round trip, as a passenger in a new TF, and thus was he smitten with the incurable disease in question.

The first car he ever bought was a TD. By the time he picked up that copy of the *Montreal Star* he'd also bought a TF 'for my wife Dorothy' which was in rotten order so he was busy restoring that, plus an MGB GT also 'for my wife Dorothy' who, he claims, was as enthusiastic as her husband about MGs.

Anyway, Barc flew over to Montreal to see the TC which was described as being in good condition. He took his tools with him, checked out the car, bought it and, next morning, set off to drive 1000 miles in two days with duplicate tyres and various spares sticking out of the back.

The expressway out of Montreal had an elevated part with rough joints between concrete sections. The TC's flexing frame assumes good, positively fitting door latches. If not, bumpy roads can make both doors fly open, as they did in this case, leaving Barc the object of some attention from fellow road users as he struggled to close the doors and keep the car in a straight line.

Later, he noticed that the battery was overheating, and traced the fault to the voltage regulator on the dynamo. It wasn't cutting off the charge and, although he tried, Barc couldn't fix it. He had to drive the rest of the way with lights and everything electrical switched on to take the power away. The fuel pump also failed but he mended that at the roadside.

And so the police car came from Kent, the 'Garden of England', to oceanic Nova Scotia, where looking over the windscreen in fog can also be useful, and there she remains, alongside Barc's TD, the TF, the B GT, and three more TDs, without doubt the greatest concentration of the marque in that part of the world. We'll leave the last word to their owner.

'I have to admit I'm a bit crazy about MGs.'

Having studied the websites for accepted methods of ribbon attachment and polished his Y to mirror sheen, Willem van der Veer was quite excited about his role as wedding chauffeur to Majan Mijnten and Johan Heimmensen. The sun was shining at 7.30 on a January morning but it was very, very cold. If only he'd charged the battery fully, the car would have started at once and he wouldn't have come so close to heart failure. 'Bedankt' is Dutch for thanks, by the way.

Why de Dion? Wherefore Diesel?

This is the man who invented the compression-ignition engine, Herbert Ackroyd-Stuart. We call it the diesel now, but we don't usually put it in an MG.

Steam-driven carriages were no novelty on British roads by 1830. In fact, they were becoming a nuisance. It was widely felt among important old farts that the horses shouldn't be frightened this way. Steaming, aggravating, metal monsters should be confined to the railway lines now being built, and so Parliament began enacting laws which damned well put a stop to it.

Tolls on roads and bridges were raised beyond reason for horselessness, and when it was stipulated that a man with a red flag by day and a red lamp by night had to precede all self-propelled road vehicles, it was time to postpone the age of the British motor car and hand the inventive initiative to the Continentals, who had no such laws.

Even so, there remained some British engineers who would not be thwarted by mere Acts of Parliament. One such, in his pursuit of economy and efficiency, published his ideas for an ideal engine. It would work by compression ignition and would run for a week on a cup of oil or a few spoonsful of coal dust – well, nearly.

This fellow, one Herbert Ackroyd-Stuart of Bletchley, built his engine while Rudolf Diesel, the cleverest boy in the class at the Munich Polytechnic, was still thinking about his. Ackroyd-Stuart put forward his first proposals in 1886 and Hornsby's of Grantham was selling engines in 1892. Diesel published his theoretical paper in 1893 and didn't have a working engine until 1897, by which time Hugh Fortescue Locke-King of Brooklands had taken delivery of a Hornsby-Ackroyd Patent Safety Oil Traction Engine. Here was a winner, surely, but somehow Dr Diesel overtook on the inside.

And so it came to pass that we don't put gallons of ackroyd in our tanks.

CHAPTER NINE

Man Buys Car 272 Times

O n the eastern shore of Lake Huron, Ontario, lies the pretty little town of Goderich, famous for its sunsets, its beaches and its salt mine. It should also be famous for a 1938 TA, also pretty, and sharp enough to come second at the Ontario show of 1200 British cars, and expensive enough to demonstrate the devotion to his car of one Art Fitzgerald, environmental consultant, and that of his wife Mary, to him.

We begin in Montreal in 1971, when Art saw the ad in the paper and phoned. He already had an interest in MGs but had never seen a pre-war model and wanted to take a look. The seller said sure enough, but Art had better be quick because there were people coming who wanted to buy it and so it might be gone.

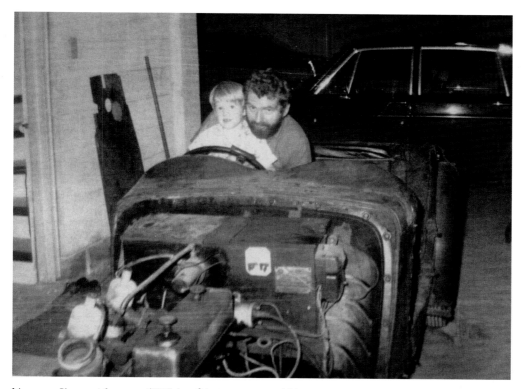

You see, I've paid a man $250 for this car, son, and I know it won't go yet, but just you wait, son. Just you wait.

Art was expecting to see a car made before the war, not necessarily one that had clearly been through all the major air raids. It had been originally registered in Leeds, Yorkshire, an industrial city which certainly had its share of bomb damage, but this was something else.

The seller was quite certain that the car had been in running order in Canada, since the 1960s, and was merely suffering from a lack of TLC. Appearances, in this case, were deceptive. Anyway, the potential buyers were expected any moment, so if that was all?

'How much do you want for it?' asked Art.

'$250,' said the seller, which was rather more than Art had to his name at the time.

'Write the cheque out, Mary,' said Art, secretly planning his tactics with the bank manager on Monday morning.

'Just a minute,' said the seller. 'What about these other people? They said they want it.'

'They might not,' said Art, 'once they've seen it. A bird in the hand saves nine stitches when the iron's hot.'

'Well, all right,' said the seller. 'I need the money. I've an old Ferrari sitting in the docks and I've got to pay import duty on it.'

I told you so.

The brakes and the steering worked but that was about all. After she was towed home, the excitement briefly faded to be replaced by the familiar 'O my lord, good heavens above, what have I been and gone and done?' But only briefly. It faded again, to be replaced by a kind of determination, patience and doggedness we can only marvel at.

As family grew up, money came and went, and different demands were made on spare time, if there was any, Art gradually restored his car to glory. 'Gradually' is the key word here. If you add 32 to 1971, you get 2003, the year in which MG TA FUM 763 was born again. During that very long time, Art reckons the expenditure on his car went from $250 to rather more, $68,000 in fact, which, if you work it backwards, represents an investment two hundred and seventy two times the down-payment. Pity really. If he'd spent just slightly less, at $2,000 a year over those 32 years, it would have been a 64,000 dollar question.

British MG overtakes
American Ford in America.

CHAPTER TEN

Searchlights Over Berlin, APB in Downey

Formed as a heavy bomber squadron in November 1942, Number 467 Squadron, Royal Australian Air Force, flew Lancasters right through the rest of the war, with much distinction and considerable losses – over 100 aircraft and crews. On the 13th November 1943 the squadron removed from its base in Bottesford, Lincolnshire, to Waddington, also Lincolnshire, and four days later a rookie crew arrived led by Pilot Officer Hugh Hemsworth, from New South Wales.

The practice at that time of the war was for the pilot of a new crew to go on two work-experience trips with one of the squadron's senior crews, which is to say longest lasting. These trips, not always welcomed by the host crew and captain thus delegated, were called 'second Dickies', the junior being second to Dicky, the

We couldn't find a picture of Hugh Hemsworth with his Lancaster. He may never have had one taken. Many bomber crews didn't, believing it to be bad luck. This is the typical scene in late 1944: an Australian contemporary, Jack Wiley, also from New South Wales (centre, middle row) with his aircrew and, front row, the ground crew who looked after 'his' Lancaster, of RAF No 9 Squadron. They also survived the war.

Unlike so many in that war, Hugh Hemsworth always came back.

captain pilot. Hemsworth's two were to Berlin, the most heavily defended city in the world.

On his first, night of 23/24 November, his own squadron had no losses but twenty two other Lancasters went down over Germany and several more crashed or crash-landed back home. It would have been a sobering introduction to bomber warfare.

The next trip was worse, with a curious tragedy to add to Hemsworth's rapidly acquired experience. Night of November 26/27 and 443 Lancasters set off for Berlin. Of these, an astonishing eighteen crashed on returning, with most crew surviving and, much less astonishing, twenty nine were lost over Germany, including one from 467 Squadron. All the crew were killed including Hemsworth's two gunners, Sergeants Sherwin and Thomas, who had been ordered to fly as 'spare bods' with that skipper, Flight Sergeant Fowler RAAF, whose usual gunners were not available.

Hemsworth came home to the news that his crew had been reduced from seven men to five before he'd had the chance to fly on ops with them himself. He managed to find a regular mid-upper (dorsal turret) gunner but never did find a constant rear gunner for the rest of his time with 467, a situation that was far from ideal. A bomber crew was a unit, with everyone relying on everyone else, and especially the tail-end Charlie who was the main man for spotting night fighters, and whose speed of reaction in ordering evasive action from his captain was a key factor in survival.

Hemsworth flew thirteen more operations with 467, including five more Berlins, before transferring with his crew to 83 Squadron, Pathfinders, in March 1944. The Pathfinder Force (PFF) squadrons didn't carry normal bombloads; their Lancasters carried parachute flares and target indicator firework bombs, to mark the target for the rest. It was a job for crews who had proved themselves to be among the

The T-ABCs For Ever club, which you can join if you have one, has members mostly in the USA, Canada, the UK and Australia, but also in Sweden, Spain, Holland, Denmark, South Africa, Germany, Switzerland, France, Phillipines, New Zealand, Uruguay, Bahamas, Portugal, Brazil, Japan, Israel, Greece, Norway, Finland, Luxembourg, Argentina, Belgium, Italy, Austria, China, India and Venezuela.

best, and the standards set for 83 Squadron were especially high, being assigned exclusively in the spring of 1944 to special ops with 5 Group, in preparation for D-Day. These ops were mainly to French targets, such as railways and munitions factories, requiring pinpoint accuracy to avoid French casualties.

Hugh Hemsworth completed his set tour of operations and could have been posted to a flying school or a desk job, but he was soon over Germany again. In October 1944 he was awarded the Distinguished Flying Cross, the citation mentioning a particular raid on Cologne but surely recognising a notable career, the most remarkable achievement of which was to get himself and his crew through alive.

Jim Shade's TC, bought new by an Australian bomber pilot in 1947, and still going strong.

Not everyone wants T series. There's a lot to be said for the A and the B.

Back in Oz in 1947, Hugh Hemsworth joined Quantas as a captain, and in March 1949 he bought an MG TC, number 7344, newly imported into Sydney. We know that he retired from Quantas in 1977, by which time an American air force bandsman called Jim Shade had left the flying types to join the police in California. He'd seen TCs and he wanted one, but the opportunity wasn't going to arise yet.

Stationed in Downey, the city with the enviable historic distinction of the oldest surviving Macdonald's restaurant, and erstwhile home to aircraft and space shuttle manufacture, Officer Shade was sitting in his patrol car when he heard an APB (All Points Bulletin – American police warning of wanted persons to be arrested) on his radio. There'd been an armed robbery at a dry cleaners. Two suspects had hijacked a car and forced the driver to help them escape (it turned out later that the designated getaway car and driver had disappeared in a panic).

Shots had been fired (accidentally, it was later realised), the kidnapped car owner had eventually been allowed free, and the suspects were hell-for-leathering it out of town. Officer Shade set off at maximum velocity, believing he had an idea where they might be headed, but pulled up when he saw two more law officers in cars at an intersection.

They were discussing the situation when the suspects' stolen car roared past. Hotly pursued, by Officer Shade right behind them in his black and white, the robber driver couldn't hold it and went into a spin. Shade blocked the suspects and confronted them, shotgun in hand. The other two officers helped out with handcuffs while Shade found the robbers' guns and a bag with $104 in it, under the front seat. The guns were stolen too.

Such high speed excitement came with the job, all the way through Jim Shade's career. He retired in 1997 as a Detective Captain, and suddenly there was no car, and no daily adrenaline. Now, at last, he could have that MG, whereupon he bought a TC that had been in California since the 1980s or possibly before, and it was number 7344. He knew nothing about her, but there was one little clue. She did have a Royal Australian Air Force Association decal on the windscreen.

Jim Shade now lives in West Covina CA, and is membership secretary of the T-ABCs For Ever club, www.mg-tabc.org, which has over 1000 members worldwide.

CHAPTER ELEVEN

The TD as Sci-Fi

TD 1034 was built in March 1950. When Denis Baggi got her in 1965, she had seats from another type of car altogether, various non-working instruments, by the look of it had had a bad accident at some point, and was painted red. Still, she ran and, despite Denis's relative lack of education in mechanical matters at that time, kept on running up and down the mountain roads of Switzerland, where Denis liked to take his holidays from his home in Lugano.

In answer to the question 'How many people can you fit in a TD?' Denis says eight students, including himself, by the village of San Bernadino, at around one thousand six hundred metres (almost five thousand feet) in 1967. The famous pass named for that village, an ancient route through the Alps from Italy, rises even higher and offers the kind of challenging twists and turns much relished by MG drivers.

There were no carphones or Twitter in those days of course, but Denis fitted a 300W short-wave radio transceiver, with which he could light a neon bulb at some distance but mainly it was to talk to fellow radio hams in Siberia, New Jersey and pretty well anywhere else.

The fun had to end when Denis was getting ready to go to Berkeley, to do his PhD in 1970. He had a friend who drove an MGB and so clearly qualified as the trustworthy sort to whom a precious TD could be sold. While Denis was away, the friend stripped the car down, discovered among many other things that the true colour was almond green, and offered to sell it back when the wanderer returned to Lugano, twenty five years later, after working in academic and industrial posts in New York and Zurich.

Denis is an owner of the evolutionary persuasion. He seeks to improve the car without compromising its originality, meaning especially its feel and its sporting purpose. If it goes faster and better than any TD ever did out of the factory, then that is something to be proud of. In any case, as he says, if owners after him wanted to remove the three temperature guages, the Tapley accelerometer, the spark-advance control on the dash, the electronic circuit in the regulator instead of the coils, the Cederstrand (*qv*) anti-sway bar on the front suspension, *et cetera et cetera*, in other words to slow the car down or make her less reliable, they could always refit her back to her drawing board design.

Purists might draw the line at the hidden five-speaker stereo, and the proximity sensor that surrounds the car with a radio bubble and sets off the alarm horn in the event of, er, well, proximity. There is no room for gloves in the glove box, it being full of LED displays for all the other sensors Denis has installed as well as the stereo amplifier.

Purists can draw whatever they like. Denis is very happy indeed, and his car goes like the wind/the clappers/a bat out of hell/greased weasel droppings (delete as applicable). The gismos are no more than a man using his knowledge, deploying it imaginatively where it hasn't been deployed before in quite this way. Denis's degree was in electrical engineering and computer science with a minor in music, and now he's a professor at the University of Applied Sciences of Southern Switzerland, with an international reputation for his research. In idle moments he has learned how to strip an engine and will be fitting an overdrive shortly.

Installing the stereo and the alarm, by the way, necessitated the introduction of a phantom negative polarity earth while maintaining the original positive earth, which is no more than you might expect from the Vice Chairman of the Institute of Electrical and Electronic Engineers Computer Society Technical Committee on Computer Generated Music.

No jokes please about cuckoo clocks and lonely goatherds. This is Denis Baggi and the fastest TD in Switzerland.

June 7, 2003, Jack Hardy drove his second daughter to her wedding to Dan Duarte. This was a very special trip for both of them, but the PA was far too small to take the newly-weds away after the celebrations. A friend of the family had a YA saloon, which was rather more made for the job.

Jonathan Fieber's 1932 C Type, photographed by Jack Hardy at the Laguna Seca MG Historic Races, near Monterey, California, 2004.

*For years
the most*
**consistently
successful**
*sports car
in the world*

safety **MG** *fast !*

THE M.G. CAR COMPANY LIMITED, SALES DIVISION, COWLEY, OXFORD
London Showroom : University Motors Ltd., Stratton House, 80 Piccadilly, W.1
Overseas Business : Nuffield Exports Ltd., Oxford and 41 Piccadilly, London, W.1

(72)

Motor magazine, October 1952.

CHAPTER TWELVE

The Heart Of The Matter

If you want to understand how cars work – that is, really understand – you won't find many better cars on which to learn than an MG. There are several reasons for this. One must be that the MG is a proper car, designed and built in the pre-computer age. There is nothing invisible, infallible, solid state nor programmable about the technology. No robots were involved in the build, and no software focus-group wind tunnel common denominators had any influence.

Two must be that the priorities in the MG design office were speed and slightly devilish excitement for the driver, rather than reliability, economy, spacious family accommodation and other such domestic virtues.

It is perhaps indicative of the MG age that no teams of international lawyers and branding consultants were assembled to report that 'mga' means haemorrhoids in at least two Inuit languages and so the label MG must be dropped in favour of GM.

Let us then consider why the MG does not appeal to everyone and, in so doing, let us identify three sorts of people in the world. There are those people who will suffer by sea or lake in rain and hail to catch a fish and cook it on an open fire, and never mind the burnt bits and the raw bits. Then, there are those who quite like that idea in theory, but don't like it enough to actually do it. And there are those who are happy cooking fish fingers from frozen in the microwave. That's the difference. Well, a difference anyway.

One of the world's rain-and-hail fishermen is Bob Muenchausen, a southern Californian, and so from a territory of the world that has embraced the automobile for as long as such embraces have been possible. Bob grew up to the sights of XK Jag, Austin Healey, Alfa Romeo, Ferrari, MG T series. They were commonplace in the post-war years. Bob says that Californians today may be having second thoughts about their affair with the automobile, and its impact on the environment and the culture, but that's now, and a political problem of masses and majorities. He's interested in then, and a kind of individuality that's worth working for.

As a youth with a new driving licence, Bob Muenchausen decided not to follow Eddie Cochrane (*The car's out front and it's all mine, Just a '41 Ford, not a '59*) because he thought that the obvious thing to do was buy a 1961 Triumph TR-3A. The TR, he says, 'was little more than a hot-rodded buckboard', but it did show him what driving could be like. Those who find it hard to imagine a hot-rodded buckboard should remind themselves of Dinah Shore singing *Buttons and Bows*:

My bones denounce the buckboard's bounce
And the cactus hurts my toes.

Bob Muenchausen's toe was flat on the floor of his TR-3A when the traffic lights changed, leaving the smoke of burned rubber on the road and many older drivers in his wake, doubtless hoping that he'd grow out of it eventually. Which, of course, he did, moving on to the more sophisticated, refined and altogether more civilised and gentlemanly sport of driving an MGA in 1966. In its turn, this purchase posed the usual dilemma: does one hire a mechanic under contract, or does one get among it oneself?

Bob took the latter course. 'There are many ways to approach a problem but the best, especially if it's an MG problem, is with an open mind. Nobody has a monopoly on MG insight and, once we realise that, we can see that it's possible to draw from many sources and to use many differing means to find an answer. Sometimes, the alternative doesn't work out so well as the traditional method. Or, we discover something better. In my own case, certain aspects of an MG's workings seemed incomprehensible at first but I came to understand SU carburettors and nothing seemed beyond me after that.'

As well as a personal journey for the owner, Bob reckons the car is making a journey too. He argues that technology moves on, and you can choose to ignore its progress or not. If the flat-earthers want to delve ever deeper into the origins of MGs and into what were the intentions, as well as the achievements, of the Abingdon engineers and designers, that's fine by Bob. But even those same engineers and designers took advantage of the changing technology of their times, reflecting the best practices of their day as they saw them.

As Bob says: 'In my opinion, we who choose to modify our MGs are trying to keep our cars moving forward through time, but all of us who drive these cars, purists or modernisers, must be benefitting the marque, because I see many more MGs on the road and at shows than other cars of their vintage.'

Two of the MGAs have gone and Bob is now content in his heart with just one – his 1968 MGB GT. 'I purchased this beast back in the fall of 1986 with, I guess, the intention of recapturing a part of my youth (I was 40 then). It took two and a half years to bring her back to something like her original glory and that was a great experience. Like every other MGB owner who has reclaimed a car by restoration, I learned a lot, not only about the car and the company's history, but about mechanics, bodywork, upholstery, and all the skills necessary to complete the job in my own garage. And, like many others, I think I learned just a little about myself as well. I suppose that might be why I bought this car back after selling it in the early 1990s, because I had so much of myself invested in it.'

Bob says he never had the resources to go too deeply into the engineering, nor to get someone else to do it, 'but there are incremental improvements and changes that a person of limited means can do, and these are what I pursued. Things like installing relays for the headlights, relays for the turn signals (to extend the life of the turn-signal switch), a modified and then an alternative heater valve, and a different alternator for better performance not only in winter, but in the electrical system all year long.'

So, Bob Muenchausen, like others in these pages, is an evolutionary. 'I think that is what the MG marque has always inspired many owners to do, to move the car along and so improve the breed.'

An old Australian second-hand car dealer called Baron, known as Munch to his friend, was lying, dying, when he picked himself up on one elbow and said 'Paint me MGs in puce, Bruce, paint me MGs in puce. They're of no further use, Bruce, so paint me MGs in puce.' And with that he breathed his last. Bruce did as bidden and, for good measure, put a sign in the showroom window: Buy One, Get One Free.

Along came a fellow and did just that. He and his son drove the cars home, resprayed them white and black, and took them out for a drive. They hadn't got very far when both cars broke down simultaneously. Bouncing down the road came a kangaroo wearing goggles, a baggy green cap and, tied raffishly round his neck, a silk scarf in the egg-and-bacon colours of the Marylebone Cricket Club.

'What's up, doc?' said the kangaroo, whipping a camera from his pouch and taking a picture of the cars.

'We've broken down,' said the man. 'I think we've got phantom negative polarity earths. No idea where they came from. Maybe they fell from that coolabah tree.'

'No worries, mate,' said the kangaroo, searching inside his pouch for his earth polarity degauger. Singing 'I should be so lucky' softly to himself, the kangaroo got busy under the bonnets and soon had those engines running again.

With a cheery wave of his paw, the kangaroo bounced off into the forest. 'Strewth,' said the fellow. 'I wonder where I can buy one of those degaugers.'

Looking superb in the Danish sunshine, two fine TCs.

CHAPTER THIRTEEN

Tom Pike's Tale of a TC And Another: Part One

Memories of my interesting cars split into two categories: driving experiences, and challenges of maintenance and repair. Over six decades, I especially remember lying on my back underneath them, replacing something critical. I remember the unique undersides of my cars just as clearly as their exteriors and interiors:

- The fins on the aluminum oil pans of my 1948 TC, usually with drops of oil at each end;
- The mechanical brake system of the 1927 La Salle convertible;
- four VW buses ('59, '61, '67, '72) with rear engines, three of which I rebuilt at some point;
- The 1959 Lancia Aurelia B20 coupé with a temperamental hydraulic clutch;
- The broken overdrive transmission of a 1958 Triumph TR3;
- The blue 1962 BMW 2002 whose muffler and shock absorbers needed replacing;
- The 1981 Lancia Zagato with leaking seals in its power rack and pinion steering;

......and the 1967 Alfa Romeo Spider needing clutch work and a new muffler. *(Editorial note: for those non-Americans of sheltered upbringing, we should point out that 'muffler' is the American term for a car's silencer. Tom Pike is not implying that his cars needed new woollen scarves).*

My father was a major influence on my interest in cars, as well as engendering the pleasure I still take in making and fixing things. Pop taught me how to use tools of all kinds by having me help him with projects. At the age of ten, I helped him construct a pre-fabricated Sears Roebuck garage and then convert it into a two-stall barn for horses. A Sears garden tractor was bought disassembled to save money and I helped Pop put it together, and shared the pleasure of its maiden run. Using the tractor to cut four acres of lawn and pasture was less fun, but keeping it in working order was good training for maintaining cars.

Pop loved the 1927 La Salle convertible I bought in 1956. I drove it from California to Kentucky when I came home that summer from college. It was red, with black top and fenders, tall wire wheels with a spare mounted on each front fender, and a rumble seat and compartment for golf clubs in back. *(Another note for those non-Americans of sheltered upbringing: 'fender' here means mudguard and not a low metal surround for the hearth).* The LaSalle was an impressive vehicle, but I sold it to get money to buy a real sports car. I wanted an MG TC.

A friend who owned a Cadillac Allard took me with him to meetings of the newly-organised local chapter of the Sports Car Club of America. While the Allard was fun (and

24 *The* Motor   *July 14, 1936.*

THE MG MIDGET SERIES 'T'

Buy a car made in the United Kingdom.

Bigger, faster, more indomitable still — this new M.G. Midget Series T! Increased to 10 h.p. Terrifically strong chassis. Hydraulic braking on a par with its speed. A car with a racing pedigree, built to the last bolt as a pukka sports car. £222 ex works, in two-seater form only. Dunlop : Triplex.

THE M.G. CAR COMPANY LIMITED · ABINGDON-ON-THAMES · BERKSHIRE

T3

A30   KINDLY MENTION "THE MOTOR" WHEN CORRESPONDING WITH ADVERTISERS.

The car in the background appears to be a 1948 Plymouth four-door sedan, a contemporary of the car in the foreground.

Tom's first TC, photographed in Stanford, California, in 1956. Who needs heaters and air conditioning when you have a car that looks like this?

scary) to drive, I fell in love with the classic simplicity of one particular TC, purchased new in 1947 by a SCCA member who had raced it at Watkins Glen in the late 1940s. *(This would have been on the original course on public roads, which they stopped using after 1952 when a car crashed into spectators, killing one person and injuring others. Ed.)*

Thinking longingly about that car, I returned to California for the 1956–1957 college year and started looking. I found a well used but sound black 1948 TC with a red interior. It had no heater of course, no cruise control, air conditioning or sound system like American cars of 1957 did. I remember driving my girlfriend's mother's Oldsmobile, top down on a hot day, cold air blowing over us, not knowing that cars made outside the US didn't necessarily have such luxuries as standard.

The MG certainly didn't, but it did have the perfect proportions, sweeping fenders, tall wire wheels, long hood, plus the driving fun that makes the TC a classic sports car. I had never driven such a responsive car with its quick steering, flat cornering and, for its time, zippy performance, especially on narrow, winding, up and down roads.

I drove it hard and blew the tired engine a year later. With the help of Blower's *MG Workshop Manual* and Smith's *Tuning and Maintenance of MGs*, I rebuilt the engine, transmission and brakes. I would use the same books to guide me in restoring my second TC, forty five years on.

My college sweetheart Lucy survived two years of dating in the TC and became my wife in the summer of 1958. A year later, expecting our first child, me still a student and able to support only one car, we reluctantly parted with the TC, making an even trade for a 1958 Morris Minor Traveller.

Years passed, MG-less years. Everywhere, families grew up and left home, while MGs waited, exhausted and forgotten, on blocks in garages, for oily-fingered persons to happen along and rescue them.

Just such a car was waiting for me, without my knowing it, in a summerhouse in Connecticut. The summerhouse belonged to my son-in-law's family; the car to his late father who had bought it in England in 1956 when a student at Oxford. He used it full time for a dozen or more years until it became in need of serious work. It was put on blocks but, before the work could be done, the owner died and so the car sat in a backyard garage for twenty five years.

Covered thickly with dust, its seats and top in shreds, with remains of squirrel and mouse nests under the bonnet and cowl, it could have been described as a mess, but what I saw was a 1947 TC; sadly derelict but eminently restorable and I was going to have her. TC 2481 was a completely original home-market car, with the exception of bumpers and heater added in America. Having been coated with Vaseline, the chrome would only need to be cleaned and polished. While red paint was cracked and flaking, body parts were virtually rust free and the vulnerable fenders were straight and without dents. Restorers of old MGs expect to replace most of the wood frames of the body tubs, usually rotten but, remarkably, the fifty year old ash pieces in TC 2481's tub were still sound.

When the call came at last, I rented a fourteen-foot enclosed van and drove to Connecticut. We winched the car up ramps into the truck and secured her for the journey to her new home in Kentucky. While I had rebuilt various parts of most of my old cars, I had never before completely disassembled one and reconditioned or replaced every part, which I knew I'd have to do this time. For part two of the story, please see page sixty five.

CHAPTER FOURTEEN

Boy Grows Up to Flirt With Disaster

Hermann Egges of Oude Pekela, a small town in northern Netherlands, used to walk past all sorts of cars on his way to school but only one stood out – the MGB roadster owned by a local photographer. This was in the late 1970s, when Hermann wasn't yet ten years old, and the boy decided that, one day, he would have such a car. Right there and then, he started collecting sales material on cars – brochures picked up from the dealerships, advertisements clipped from newspapers and magazines – and this turned into a hobby.

Twenty years later, in 2001, he fulfilled his ambition with a 1977 MGB which had been imported some time before from Beverley Hills. It turned out not to be quite the dream car, giving him a number of minor problems but nothing really major and it was fine for summer weekends and jaunts with the MGCC of Holland. Above all, it provided Hermann with a lot of fun over ten years and generated in him a great

Hermann Egges in his TD, pre-restoration. He is going to do the whole thing himself, when he has time. Anyone already experienced in such a matter should contact Hermann direct with advice and encouragement.

The Autocar, October 29, 1948

Safety **MG** fast!

STAND No. 148
GROUND FLOOR
EARLS COURT

see them at the Motor Show

Here are three of the MG breed that we shall be showing at Earls Court; the MG Midget, the MG 1¼ litre Saloon and, for its first time 'out of the stable,' the new MG 1¼ litre Tourer. They've got many more interesting features than we can show you here, so be sure to come and see us at the Motor Show.

Safety **MG** fast!

THE **MG** CAR COMPANY LTD., ABINGDON - ON - THAMES   **N** NUFFIELD PRODUCTS
Overseas Business : Nuffield Exports Ltd., Oxford, and 41 Piccadilly, London, W.1

The Motor   Colour 6   October 19, 1955

1st
of a new line

TO MEET THE CHALLENGE OF TOMORROW ON ROAD & TRACK

THE COMPLETELY NEW MG SERIES **MGA**

This potential trophy-winner breaks clean away from traditional M.G. styling, yet it inherits all the qualities and fine craftsmanship that have, for over a quarter of a century distinguished its famous predecessors. Many of its features are identical to those embodied and tested in George Eyston's record-smashing M.G. Special. Faster . . . sturdier . . . safer, it holds the road like a limpet and its 1500 c.c. O.H.V. engine puts up a performance that is quite exceptional.

Safety fast !

You'll see it at the Motor Show!

The luxury saloon with the sporting pedigree also awaits your inspection — the brilliantly successful M.G. Magnette.

THE M.G. CAR COMPANY LIMITED, SALES DIVISION, COWLEY, OXFORD
London Showrooms: Stratton House, 80 Piccadilly, London, W.1
Overseas Business: Nuffield Exports Limited, Cowley, Oxford, and 41 Piccadilly, London, W.1

MG interest to mix with his other pastime, car advertising. The result is one of the most fascinating sports car websites: www.car-brochures.eu. On it are several thousand contemporary advertisements and brochures for all sorts of classic British cars, but especially MG.

Not surprisingly, Hermann has quite a few examples from the career of the T series over its nineteen years, and this type is his favourite. He's bought one, a 1951 TD, that was found in a barn in Hermosa Beach, California. Currently the car is in restoration, a long-term project for one with a busy life otherwise.

And this is where the story takes a sad turn. Married to Tineke, with two sons Tim and Hugo, the family won't fit in the B. He's sales director of a company that makes kit for the oil and gas exploration industry, and travels a lot. In nine months he visited thirteen countries. Had he but world enough, and time, this TD, Hermann, were no crime (with apologies to Andrew Marvell). These are Hermann's own words:

'I am searching for a four seater, so I am able to take the whole family with me, but I can't afford a four seater MG roadster at the moment. I have still some time but, if I'm to keep the TD, and I am, then I'm afraid my B will have to go after ten years. I'd really like a B GT but I'm thinking about a pre-war or early post-war Austin or Morris.'

Hermann. You cannot be serious.

Richard and Valerie Hartington's Maggie, in Devon sun.

CHAPTER FIFTEEN

A Restoration in Microcosm
Or, A Tale of Two Doors

Given the fondness of sports car aficionados for classic MGs, new replacements are available for virtually every part of a TC. Some are made in England, others in Europe, and increasing numbers in China and Taiwan. In my experience, about a third of the replacements I ordered were inferior to the originals, in either the quality of material or accuracy of manufacture. As I was determined that the restored TC 2481 would be as original as possible, I renovated existing worn parts whenever feasible, using the best replacements when I had to.

Restoring an old car requires a blend of fanaticism, patience, continuous problem-solving, lots of time, and money. Restoring TC 2481 took four years, beginning in 2002, but fortunately I had a good workshop, the original garage underneath the solid 1950s house designed and built by my wife's architect father. I have workbenches along one wall, storage cabinets on another and, in one of the two bays, a hydraulic lift to raise the car. My bad back much appreciates this luxury in my advanced years.

Several years of restoration prepares you for disappointments. You begin to expect things to take two or three times longer than your first estimate, and so it was as I gradually rebuilt my red devil. Even so, by February of 2006, I had a running chassis with the body tub, seats, and tub interior installed. The next challenge was getting the doors to fit and swing, a procedure which, in its detail, sums up the experience of all of us who have ever tackled an MG in its entirety.

I had hoped that, since the two doors had fitted when I took them off, they might fit when I bolted the hinges back on, but no. I hung the doors and the top front corners were half an inch too high.

As we know, doors and tub are made of thin, subtly curved steel panels bent around frames made of pieces of English ash, screwed and glued together, with a few metal reinforcements. Having spent several years in a dehumidified workshop and been painted in modern paint booths, the body parts had warped a bit.

I had been warned of the tricky nature of door alignment. The owner's manual, called the *Brown Book*, says to loosen the six bolts holding the tub on the frame, and add packing between the frame and the tub at the mounting points until you find the tub bends ever so slightly to allow both doors to fit just right.

I decided first to place packing at the tub's rear mounting points to raise the back of the tub, which would push the line of the top door hinges forward and have the desired effect of lowering the top front corners of the doors. It worked. The doors now fitted the openings, but the top hinges were bent so I couldn't shut them. Should I order replacement parts or try to rehab the old parts?

This what a 1947 TC can become by 1999, after many years in a shed in Connecticut.

And this is what she can become after four years of restoration by a dedicated enthusiast like Tom Pike. That's him, grinning like the Cheshire cat, and so he should be.

Looking at a stripped chassis can give you mixed feelings, but the only way from here is up.

I called Bobbie at Abingdon Spares in Walpole, New Hampshire – my favourite source. Most of their parts came from England, which meant they were usually good replicas of the originals, but at that time more expensive because of the weakness of the dollar against sterling and the euro. Two pairs of door hinges, the right side top, #41083 and the left side top #40831b, came in at $85.14 per pair, including new hinge pin assemblies.

They arrived two days later and turned out to vary in dimensions slightly from the originals. No good. They were a later pattern and mine was an early TC. I would have to repair the original hinges.

When I lacked the proper equipment or ran out of ideas, I called Bruce Domeck at Unique Automotive, a man who can fix just about anything on virtually any car. I took him my hinges. Inside his shop and in the parking lot was the usual menagerie of vintage Ferraris, an early Jaguar XKE, a couple of Formula Ford race cars, a 1949 MGTC he was restoring, a Triumph TR4, a 1932 Mercedes convertible, and a 1939 Ford pickup street rod. He couldn't figure out how my TC's hinges could have been so badly bent, but twenty minutes later he had straightened them on one of his presses. As soon as I got home, I hung the doors yet again.

The passenger door was perfect but the driver's door was out in three ways: gaps at the top on both hinge and handle sides, and too low in front to close. Whatever I did to fix it, I'd have to be very careful not to unfix the perfect passenger door. The gap on the hinge edge was cured by moving the hinge one-eighth of an inch towards the outside of its door. I sanded two short pieces of hardwood dowel rod to make a tight fit in the worn quarter-inch bolt holes, glued them in place and let the plugged door sit overnight for the glue to dry. Next day, I drilled new holes, bolted on the hinge, and once more hung the door.

Good. Now for the gap at the front edge which was caused by a warp in the door itself. The answer to this came from the mg-tabc Yahoo group, which has over a thousand members across the world. It happened to have several messages about curing warped doors. I adapted a tensioning rod sold in ordinary hardware stores to eliminate sagging on the screen doors of houses. After some blacksmithing, I installed the much-reduced rod diagonally across the inside of the door, re-hung it on the tub and, with a small crescent wrench, slowly tightened the turnbuckle. A quarter of a turn was all that was needed. My door was unwarped. But it was still too low in front to close properly.

I looked in the *Brown Book* for a clue and there it was – in the Coachwork chapter under 'Remounting Body …(ix) Adjustment of Door (door low) – This operation will necessitate packing under the hinge pillar'.

Here we went again. I loosened the six mounting bolts which held the body to the frame, removed the bolt from the mount next to the right side hinge pillar, placed a hydraulic jack at the rear of the body, and raised the right side about a quarter of an inch. I slid a one-sixteenth steel washer between the pieces of packing already there, replaced the bolt, retightened all the mounting bolts, let down the jack and re-hung the door.

You can't beat moments like this. You hold your breath, say a prayer to the gods of MGs, and try it. As the handsome prince said when he placed the glass slipper on the delicate foot of Cinderella, 'It fits, it fits.'

Of course, there is an important point to all this. It's not just an obsession, a willingness to go to any lengths to get things right. The reason is the pleasure of owning and driving a car of such beauty and character. So far I have had four years of driving the old girl, now aged sixty four, and she makes me feel fifty years younger, so who's going to argue with that?

Representing Denmark, on the right is Jeroen Duys with his ivory 1947 TC, and on the left his father Ludo with his 1946 version. Jeroen's is restored; Ludo's has been maintained and repaired over many years.

The Autocar

27 August 1954

Congratulations to

M.G. CARS LIMITED

AND TO **CAPTAIN G. E. T. EYSTON** ON HIS WORLD

RECORD-BREAKING SUCCESSES AT SALT LAKE FLATS, UTAH

INTERNATIONAL CLASS F				AMERICAN NATIONAL CLASS F		
	RECORD	PREVIOUS RECORD			RECORD	PREVIOUS RECORD
10 MILES	153.69 m.p.h.	135.33 m.p.h.		**10** MILES	153.69 m.p.h.	No record
500 MILES	120.30 m.p.h.	114.29 m.p.h.		**300** MILES	121.02 m.p.h.	103.24 m.p.h.
1,000 KILOMETRES	120.92 m.p.h.	115.69 m.p.h.		**400** MILES	119.98 m.p.h.	100.97 m.p.h.
1,000 MILES	120.13 m.p.h.	107.30 m.p.h.		**500** KILOMETRES	121.08 m.p.h.	No record
2,000 KILOMETRES	120.19 m.p.h.	105.47 m.p.h.		**500** MILES	120.62 m.p.h.	99.48 m.p.h.
3 HOURS	120.91 m.p.h.	114.52 m.p.h.		**1,000** KILOMETRES	121.22 m.p.h.	64.83 m.p.h.
6 HOURS	121.42 m.p.h.	114.74 m.p.h.		**1,000** MILES	120.30 m.p.h.	64.84 m.p.h.
12 HOURS	120.74 m.p.h.	105.48 m.p.h.		**2,000** KILOMETRES	120.34 m.p.h.	No record
				3 HOURS	121.38 m.p.h.	65.82 m.p.h.
				6 HOURS	121.63 m.p.h.	65.69 m.p.h.
				12 HOURS	120.87 m.p.h.	65.08 m.p.h.

Subject to official confirmation.

WE ARE PROUD TO HAVE MADE THE PANELS AND ASSEMBLED THEM
TO THE BODY FRAME AND CHASSIS OF THE RECORD-BREAKING CAR

MIDLAND SHEET METAL WORKS LTD.

BULL RING, CHILVERS COTTON, NUNEATON

Telephone: NUNEATON 3209

High-grade panel work and panel pressings for the motor industry

Hail to the Captain

If there was ever an archetypal English racing driver from those glamorous earlier days of scarves and goggles, it would have to be George Edward Thomas Eyston, born 28 June 1897. His father's occupation is listed as 'gentleman', which is to say that Edward R J Eyston had no need to work, so he didn't, but there's more to it than that. The Eystons were a significant family, having held the lordship of the manor of East Hendred, Berkshire (now Oxfordshire), Vale of the White Horse, near Didcot, and occupied the same manor house, for over 500 years (now 600 of course – they're still there).

The boy George was the elder of two sons so he might have been expected to await his inheritance in idle fashion, while Eyston Minor prepared for the church or the army. Eyston Major, though, had a gift for mathematics and a consuming interest in mechanics. After school at Stonyhurst College, he went up to Trinity College, Cambridge, to read engineering.

The First World War put a stop to that. George joined the Dorsets in the most junior officer rank, second lieutenant, whence he was removed to the Royal Artillery where, his senior officers presumed, his knowledge of practical matters would better serve his King. We don't know if they were right or wrong about that, but we do know that George was awarded the Military Cross, was mentioned in despatches twice, was wounded at Arras, and came out of the war, having been in France for virtually the whole of it, as a captain.

That was not a particularly high rank for four years in an army that had continuously lost officers in horrifying numbers, which rather suggests he was more interested in work than promotion. Certainly he went back to Trinity as soon as he could, where he became another sort of captain, of the college rowing club, and just missed out on a blue.

With a degree but no real impetus towards anything in particular, he happened to be on holiday in France in 1921, near Le Mans, when the Grand Prix was to be run. Out of curiosity, George went along and saw the American, Jimmy Murphy, win in a Duisenberg when he had been twelfth on the grid, while another American, Ralph DePalma had been first but finished second in a Ballot. DePalma was famous for winning many other races but perhaps more so for another one he didn't win, the 1912 Indianapolis 500 when, in the lead, an oil leak caused a total conk-out a mile from the line. He and his mechanic, Rupert Jeffkins, pushed her home but were overtaken, and disqualified anyway.

Eyston, having seen the epic battle at Le Mans, was smitten with the whole thing but especially with speed. He'd come on holiday in a GN cyclecar, which had a notional top speed of 60mph to be achieved with rare difficulty but would generally tootle along rather more sedately.

The world land-speed record at this time, set in 1914, was 124mph. Murphy had averaged around 79mph to win his French Grand Prix, 30 laps, total distance 320 miles or so. DePalma averaged 74mph coming in a quarter of an hour behind (more than two laps) and the third man, Jules Goux, also in a Ballot, was six minutes behind that at 72mph. Henry Segrave who, in only six years' time, would become the first human to drive a car at 200mph, was ninth, an hour behind Murphy in a Sunbeam.

Speed, of course, is relative. Doing 80 or 90 in a 1921 Ballot would be somewhat more sensational than 500mph in a 2011 Boeing.

George Eyston bought himself a second-hand Sunbeam racer when he got home. With knowledge of a car's mechanics being at least as important as driving skill if you wanted to get around the laps and win, Eyston, now known to everyone as The Captain, set about stripping cars and rebuilding them. He met Lionel Martin of Bamford and Martin, who made Aston Martin cars, and was offered a drive at Brooklands, Whitsuntide 1923. He won two races and came second in two more.

Eyston drove many marques of racing car, including Bugatti. Elsewhere it is stated that he won the 1926 French Grand Prix in a Bugatti. A Bugatti did win it, one of only three cars to start, but George wasn't driving in the race. He did win Grands Prix – there were about thirty such races that did not count towards the World Championship, which then consisted

1932 K1, a type certainly driven by Eyston, but here doing nothing other than looking magnificent by the waterside.

only of the Spanish, Italian, British and official French Grands Prix plus the Indy 500. George won at Boulogne 1926 and at La Baule on sand in 1927.

He was third on the grid in the 1926 British Grand Prix at Brooklands but retired after 45 of 110 laps in his Aston Martin, with a blown gasket. The next year at the British, he retired after 95 of 125 laps with a failed supercharger in his Bugatti, but George never seemed to stick with the same thing for very long. He'd win the 100mph Short Handicap at a charity meeting, beating Frazer-Nash and Riley in 1927, then he'd pop up winning a race at Ards in a Lea-Francis. In an Alfa Romeo he came third in the 1933 French Grand Prix; he also drove Maserati, Bentley, Riley, Stutz and others.

His name goes more closely with MG because of races won and records set, starting in the early 1930s. He became a real celebrity in motoring circles in December 1930, when he drove the MG Magic Midget, the EX120 (a much modified M type) to a new speed record, 100mph in a 750cc car (actually 103.13), on the Montlhéry circuit near Paris.

It was decided to fit a Powerplus supercharger, which Eyston had helped design, so they could go for another record, for distance and speed together: to cover 100 miles in a 750cc car in an hour, also at Montlhéry. Eyston was almost at the end of his hour, or so he thought, when the Magic Midget caught fire. English aristocrat-hero that he was, the record had to come first so, upper lip stiff as you like, he put her in neutral, in case he could coast far enough to make the 100 miles.

When the flames found him in the cockpit and set his seat on fire, he realised that the game was up, but he couldn't stop the car because the brake pedal was red hot and his shoes were burning. Climbing out onto the back, by now doing about 60, he could just reach the steering wheel, so he aimed for the grass verge and jumped when he got there.

'What a rude shock on landing,' he wrote later. 'The mere 50 or 60mph seemed nothing in the driver's seat, but when I decanted myself the impact was rather startling.'

MG

Maintaining the Breed

MG 10-9

Bred true to type, the MG Midget T.C. Series possesses all the stamina and resilience of its predecessors. Chief among its many virtues are lively acceleration, lightning response to controls, superb braking power and inherent roadworthiness.
Price £412. 10. 0 ex works plus Purchase Tax £115. 6. 8

Safety fast!

THE MG CAR COMPANY LTD. ABINGDON-ON-THAMES, BERKS.

His overalls were alight and there was nothing left of his shoes and socks. He was headed for a fortnight in hospital and three months' convalescence, but the good news was that he'd made the record. He'd achieved 100 miles in an hour on the lap before. The fire was obviously caused by over-doing it.

His next record attempt featured an asbestos suit of his own design, which he tested for the press by having people try to burn him with blowlamps.

Motor racing was being dominated by Italians, French, Americans, everybody except the British, so MG entered a team of Magnettes for the Mille Miglia. During night practice, Eyston drove through a set of level-crossing gates but that was a minor matter. The favourite for the race was the Maserati team, but MG had a cunning plan.

Another well known driver, Tim Birkin, was to go all-out in the early stages to force the Maserati drivers into putting too much strain on their cars trying to keep up. They fell for it. Although Birkin's car also proved unable to keep up the pace, the other two MGs, driven by Eyston and Johnny Lurani, Earl Howe and Hugh Hamilton, came through from behind and won the Mille Miglia team prize.

More records were broken by Eyston than by anyone before him, and in all sorts of cars including diesels that he designed and built himself, and MGs naturally, but MG unfortunately couldn't help him with some of the things he wanted to do. There was 'Speed of the Wind', an advanced, streamlined machine powered by a V-12 Rolls-Royce Kestrel, which he drove in July 1936 to the world hour record at 162 miles.

This led to the 'Thunderbolt', with two supercharged Kestrels in a six-wheeled monster of his own design and build. In 1937 and 1938, at Bonneville, he broke the world land speed record three times, at 311mph, 345mph and 357mph, briefly interupted by John Cobb in the Railton Special.

During the Second World War, Eyston worked for the Ministry of Production and later became a director of Castrol. He still took part in record attempts as a manager and adviser for MG and Austin Healey, and received the OBE from King George VI, although not the knighthood that he would certainly have had today. The grand old man of British motor racing died in a railway carriage, travelling up to London from Winchester, 11 June1979.

He always believed that racing improved the breed: 'Motor racing is a man's game, calling for iron nerves and quick action. To those of us who practise it the starter's flag is a lovely sight, but do not run away with the idea that the speed man is a reckless, daring individual who sneers at the principles of Safety First. He practises them all the time. He never takes an avoidable risk, and even when the great lust of speed comes over him when he is engaged in a hard fight with another competitor, he must preserve that mental equipoise which will enable him to weigh chances in the balance. True, it is a fine balance, in which a grain of indiscretion might mean disaster. It would be ridiculous to say that motor racing is not a risky game — of course it is. But empires have been won because men have taken risks.'

CHAPTER SIXTEEN

The Vatman's Revenge

Mike Wilde is a patient sort of a fellow – and meticulous. In his professional life, he builds up cases against major tax defrauders, big companies that employ very clever accountants who find ways of avoiding Value Added Tax or, sometimes, who devise schemes for claiming massive amounts back on non-existent goods. Staring at figures all day long, trying to espy a little inconsistency that might lead to a big hole in the wall, not surprisingly leads to a wish for some excitement outside office hours.

Normally, this is easily supplied. A couple of halves of mild ale at the local pub and the cricket highlights on the TV are quite enough – or at least they were, until an urge to get an MG took a hold of his spirit.

Mike is not mechanically minded. He did not want to spend his spare waking hours lying beneath an antique that dripped black gunge on him. He believed he could find that same excitement in driving, that excitement of old and so closely associated with the MG marque, in one of the new models.

We must make it clear that what follows is not a criticism of modern MGs in any way, nor have we made an exception to our rule (no post-Abingdon MGs) in order to poke fun at the inheritors of the sacred initials. This story is obviously a one-off, a confluence of accident, fate, ill fortune and bad luck that could never be repeated. It could have been any kind of car. It just happened to be a ZR 120.

The car was purchased on 24 March 2003. The first real outing was from Mike's home in Buxton, Derbyshire, to the Lake District with his wife Ann on 8 April. On arrival at their hotel an investigation, caused by the illuminated oil indicator, revealed that all the engine oil had disappeared. Mike filled her up and returned his new pride and joy to the dealer, April 10th.

The problem lay with the piston rings, badly fitted at the factory, allowing oil to be burned in the cylinder head. Such an eventuality had not been envisaged by the authorities; there were no new piston rings available anywhere. For the rest of that month, all of May and most of June, Mike had to make do with a succession of courtesy cars but, at last, the dealer's sales manager happened to be at a conference in Scotland and was moaning about Mike's piston rings. A Scots colleague suggested a possible source and they found some in Glasgow.

The engine was rebuilt and the ZR 120 came home on 20 June. Everything seemed OK, and for a few days it still was, until an idiot parked a VW camper van at the top of the hill – quite a steep hill – where Mike lived. He hadn't been able to put his car in the garage that day because another, different, idiot had parked in front, so the MG was at the roadside. The elderly VW camper had a badly maintained and insecure hippy-type hand-brake, insufficient for holding it still on those hard, uncool inclines such as they have in the Derbyshire peaks, and so it was that it

Don't look so happy, Mike. You're about to discover nothing where there should be engine oil.

rolled away, unattended, bouncing from lamp post to pillar box. Mike heard the racket and reached his sitting room window just in time to see the van deliver a heavy, glancing blow to his car.

The driver's door and much of the offside bodywork was crushed; the dealer collected the car on a low loader that same day, 28 June. Mike told the story in the pub to his friends, who would now look forward to his nightly arrival in expectation of yet another amusing episode in the MG saga. They would not be disappointed for long.

The car came back on the low loader on 10 July. Mike watched the delivery with a strange feeling of premonition, and winced in sympathetic but unsurprised pain as the car, misdirected by the low-loading unloading person, hit its front skirt on the kerb and crumpled it. Back she went, to be returned this time by the bodyshop's authorised driver. After he'd gone, Mike noticed a lot of extra miles on the clock and some scuffed alloy and oil deposits on the headlining. All knowledge of these matters was denied by those who were the only ones who could have been responsible but, as a quid pro quo, or an admission of guilt without actually admitting anything, Mike was able to negotiate a free servicing deal for the rest of the three year warranty.

MG went into administration in April 2005 and the warranty became worthless. Still, having got this far, Mike was determined to enjoy this blasted car and so he did, for another two years, until August 2007 when the engine blew at 42,000 miles. He had a reconditioned one fitted and part-exchanged his MG for a Peugeot.

A thing of beauty is a joy for ever, and so is a Chandler.

CHAPTER SEVENTEEN

Le Professeur, Sans Doute Craqué Pour MG

After misspending his youth like so many of us, but specialising in jazz, progressive rock, science fiction and crime novels, Professor Jean-Paul Donnay of the Department of Geomatics, University of Liège, settled down to an orthodox life as researcher and teacher. He ran a second-hand Mini, met a girl called Marie-Louise, better known as Papou, who had a new yellow one. They married in 1977 and lived happily ever after.

Hey there, just a minute, isn't there something in between? Jean-Paul?

'Mais oui. La première voiture neuve que j'ai pu payer de mes propres deniers (1979) était une très jolie Alfa Sud Sprint 1500.' (The first new car I could buy with my own money was a very pretty Alfa Sud Sprint 1500.) 'Malheureusement, elle s'est avérée peu fiable, et sa carrosserie est très rapidement partie en dentelle.' (Unfortunately, it proved unreliable, and its bodywork soon turned into lacework.)

'Refroidi par cette expérience, je me suis contenté par la suite de voitures réputées (et réputées seulement) raisonnables et solides: VW Golf et Passat, et plus récemment une Audi A3 dont certains aspects me réconcilient un peu avec les voitures modernes.' (Put off by this experience, I stuck with cars known (and known only) as sensible and sound: VW Golf and Passat and, more recently, an Audi A3 which partly won me over to modern cars.)

'Je restais pourtant fasciné par les Jaguar, Maserati, Lotus ou Triumph – pour ne citer que quelques marques – des années 60 et 70, et j'ai même fait une sorte de fixation sur la Morgan durant quelques années.' (I was still fascinated by Jaguar, Maserati, Lotus or Triumph – to quote only a few marques – from the 60s and 70s, and I even became a little in love with Morgans for a few years.)

'J'assistais à quelques manifestations (plutôt rares à l'époque), j'achetais régulièrement des revues consacrées aux voitures anciennes et je suivais les cotes du marché. Mais c'était l'époque où il fallait fréquemment conduire les enfants (deux garçons, Lionel 1980 et Maxime 1987) à l'école et où, professionnellement, j'étais amené à utiliser beaucoup plus souvent mon véhicule qu'aujourd'hui, principalement en circuits urbains et autoroutiers.' (I went to a few shows (rather rare at the time), I regularly bought magazines devoted to classic cars and I followed the market prices. But I had two children to take to school (boys Lionel 1980 and Maxime 1987) and I had to use my car much more often professionally than I do now, mainly in town and on motorways.)

'Fin de l'année 2000, mon laboratoire déménage au sein de l'université. Mon collègue, et nouveau voisin de palier, François Ronday, s'avère grand amateur d'anciennes voitures anglaises. Il possède une TR6 et une MGB, qu'il préfère.' (In

Baby, you can drive my car, as Jean-Paul said to Papou.

The ideal car for the Riviera, don't you think?

All the way from the USA.

The Belgian version.

2000, my laboratory moved to the main campus of the university. My colleague and new next-door neighbour, François Ronday, a great enthusiast for classic British cars, had a TR6 and an MGB, which he preferred.)

'On en discute souvent et, dès le printemps, il me fait essayer la MG décapotée. Et là, c'est le coup de foudre! Jusque là, je n'avais qu'un intérêt modéré pour les MG, préférant les carrosseries plus spectaculaires. (We often talked cars and, in the spring, he let me have a go in the MG, top down. The scales fell from my eyes. Until then, I'd had only a moderate interest in MGs, preferring the more flashy body styles.)

'Mais tout d'un coup, la MGB me passionne. Facile et agréable à conduire, moteur performant avec une belle sonorité, mécanique simple et accessible, ligne pure et intemporelle.' (But all at once the MGB became my fascination: easy and fun to drive, powerful engine with a spellbinding sound, mechanically simple and accessible, clean and timeless line.)

'Bon, mon collègue m'aurait fait essayé sa TR6, j'aurais sans doute craqué pour la Triumph de la même manière. Mais la MGB est la sportive qui a été la plus construite et, par conséquent, on en trouve aisément sur le marché de l'occasion à des prix abordables, et toutes les pièces de rechange sont accessibles, selon mon collègue.' (Sure, if my colleague had given me his TR6 to try, I would have fallen for it in the same way. But the MGB was the biggest selling classic sports car; it was widely available on the second-hand markets at affordable prices, and spares were easy to find, according to my colleague.)

'Cette fois c'est décidé, je vais m'en trouver une. Et toute la famille m'y encourage. Je n'ai pas à aller bien loin. À un kilomètre de chez moi, se trouve le garage Devillers, ancien représentant Mini et Rover, mais travaillant sur toutes les anciennes anglaises. Je l'ai déjà visité à plusieurs reprises pour me renseigner sur une Triumph ou une Lotus exposée en vitrine et mise en vente pour un client, mais sans jamais donner suite.' (Decision made. I must have one. And the whole family was with me on this. I had not far to go. One kilometre from my house was the Devillers garage, former agent for Mini and Rover, repairers for all the classic English cars. I'd been there often enough to make enquiries about a Triumph or a Lotus they'd put in their showroom for one of their clients, but I'd never taken it further.)

'Quand je lui parle de ma ferme intention d'acquérir une MGB, il me met en garde contre les vices cachés des anciennes européennes (carrosserie en particulier) et me suggère d'envisager la rénovation complète d'une MG importée des USA.' (When I told the man I was set on buying an MGB, he warned me against the hidden defects I might find with an old one bought locally, especially in the coachwork, and suggested I consider a B imported from the USA, which his firm would renovate.)

'Il me montre quelques unes des rénovations qu'il a réalisées pour ses clients. Elles sont superbes et toutes différentes. C'est que le client élabore une rénovation 'à la carte' et, s'il le souhaite, il peut participer activement à la rénovation.' (He showed me some of the renovations they'd done, all beautiful, and all different because the client can specify a custom renovation. Also, I could play a real part in the job.)

'C'est exactement ce qu'il me faut: je pourrai décider de chaque détail, et j'aurai le temps de me remettre progressivement à la mécanique en suivant la rénovation étape par étape. Il faut dire que si j'ai pas mal bricolé mes toutes premières voitures d'occasion lorsque j'étais étudiant (Simca 1000 et Mini), je n'ai plus touché à un moteur depuis un quart de siècle' (This suited me perfectly. I could decide every detail, and I'd have time to get back to mechanics gradually, following the renovation step by step. I should say that although I tinkered quite a bit with my cars when I was a student (Simca 1000 and Mini), I had not touched a motor for a quarter century.'

'En mai 2002, on me signale une importation en cours d'une MGB 1978 ou 1979 provenant de Californie. Elle serait saine mais dans un état peu engageant. Quand elle arrive début juillet, il faut vraiment avoir la foi pour me décider à l'acheter: capote en lambeaux, sièges déchirés, peinture complètement lessivée, petites bosses à gauche et à droite, accessoires manquants, moteur sale avec l'enchevêtrement du système de dépollution US. Mais apparemment pas de rouille et complète quant aux éléments principaux, et même un beau porte-bagages chromé original.' (In May 2002, I was told about an MGB 1978 or 1979 to be imported from California, in reasonable health but unlovely to look at. When it arrived in early July, I really needed faith in the project to buy it: tattered hood, torn seats, paint completely washed out, small bumps on the left and right, bits missing, dirty engine with the complications of the American emissions system. Otherwise, no rust and all main elements present, even a nice original chrome luggage rack.)

'Alors je paie la carcasse. Première grande question: vais-je entamer une rénovation dans le respect du véhicule original, ou vais-je me faire plaisir en la personnalisant? Les MGB de la fin des années 70 prévus pour le marché américain présentent plusieurs avantages: culasse sans plomb, allumage électronique, servo-frein, refroidissement avec vase d'expansion et double ventilateur, barres stabilisatrices, etc.' (So, I bought the carcass. First big question: should I go for renovation as per original vehicle, or should I have fun customising? The late 70s B for the US market had several benefits: OK for unleaded petrol, electronic ignition, servo brakes, cooling with expansion tank and dual fan, stabiliser bars, etc.)

'Mais les gros pare-chocs, le gros carburateur et le système de dépollution, l'absence de radiateur d'huile et les finitions en plastique de qualité douteuse ne me plaisent pas du tout.' ('But the big bumpers, big carburettor and pollution control system, the lack of oil cooler and the plastic finishings of dubious quality did not please me at all.')

'Alors je choisis de lui donner l'aspect extérieur de la version Mk II des années 1967–69, avec grille et pare-chocs chromés et, tant qu'on y est, avec des jantes à rayons, tandis que le moteur sera remis dans l'état des versions européennes de la fin des années 70, sans système de dépollution et avec la double carburation SU. En outre, on installera un overdrive et un radiateur d'huile.' (I chose to give her the appearance of the Mark II (1967–69), with grille and chrome bumpers and, while we were at it, wire wheels. The engine would be as European versions of the late 70s, without the pollution control system and with the twin SU carburettors. In addition, we'd have overdrive and oil cooler.)

'Pour l'intérieur, le tableau de bord et son instrumentation seront conservés mais avec un placage de bois et l'habitacle sera refait en cuir et vinyle. Cela fait beaucoup de boulot, en particulier du travail de carrosserie sur lequel je suis totalement incapable d'intervenir.' (For the interior, the dashboard and its instrumentation would be retained but with wood veneer, and the upholstery would be in leather and vinyl. This would entail a lot of work, particularly on the body, which was way outside my own ability.)

'La rénovation de la carrosserie confiée à Éric Devillers ne pourra pas commencer avant la fin de l'été. Mais en attendant, je prépare le terrain et commence un log-file, sorte d'agenda où je vais consigner toutes les opérations (visites au garage, achats, travaux, séances de photos) au jour le jour durant toute la période de rénovation.'

How it was, how it was naked and, opposite, what it became.

(The renovation of the body, entrusted to Eric Devillers, could not begin before the end that summer. By way of preparation, I set up a log on computer, a kind of diary in which I would record everything – visits to the garage, purchases, jobs, photo shoots – daily throughout the renovation period.)

'Je demande un certificat du BMIHT pour obtenir tous les détails sur le véhicule et je fais la liste des principales pièces de rechange à acquérir. Je ne connais pas encore bien la MGB et il faut que je me documente au maximum – quelques ouvrages de référence mais surtout une très large consultation du Web.' (I needed a BMIHT certificate for full vehicle details and a list of major replacement parts to buy. I was not very familiar with the MGB; I needed to study everything I could find, including reference books and anything on the internet.)

'L'usage d'Internet me permet également de commander les pièces neuves auprès des sites anglais, et je m'inscris au MGOC dès octobre pour bénéficier des avantages de leur catalogue et de leurs conseils en ligne.' (Through the internet I could order new parts from English sites, and I registered with MGOC during October so I'd have the benefits of their catalogue and online advice.)

'Au fur et à mesure du démontage de la voiture pour la préparer le travail de carrosserie, je reprends à domicile toutes les pièces mécaniques et accessoires que je peux rénover: nettoyage, démontage, réparation ou remplacement, polissage. Tout l'automne 2002 et l'hiver 2003 vont y passer. Je passe chez le carrossier deux ou trois fois par semaine pour reprendre et ramener des pièces, et suivre la rénovation de la carrosserie. Elle a été ramenée à la tôle, réparée et surfacée. Il est temps de choisir la couleur.' (As the car was dismantled to prepare for the body rebuild, I took home all the mechanical parts and accessories that I could restore myself, for cleaning, disassembly, repair or replacement, polishing. The autumn of 2002 and the winter of 2003 came and went. I popped in to the body repair shop two or three times a week to pick up and return parts and to check on progress of body renovation. They took it down to the metal, repaired and primed. It was time to choose the colour.)

'J'hésite entre un bleu royal et un vert 'mallard' (col-vert), deux teintes originales de chez Triumph utilisées sur les MG durant les années 70. Grosse discussion à la maison, mais je finis par choisir le vert mallard qui présente des variations entre le vert très foncé et le bleu selon l'illumination. Cela me fait penser aux couleurs de la malachite.' (I hesitated between Royal Blue and Mallard Green, two original colours from Triumph but used on MG during the 70s. Big discussion at home, but I ended up choosing the mallard, a very dark green which can look blue-ish in certain lights. It reminded me of the colours of the green mineral, malachite.)

'Dès la peinture terminée, commence le remontage de la mécanique et des accessoires. Pour l'intérieur, ce sera beige: cuir pour les sièges avec repose-tête et l'accoudoir, vinyle pour les garnitures et un épais tapis beige un peu plus foncé sur le fond. La nouvelle capote en mohair aura également un ciel de couleur beige. La combinaison du vert mallard et des beiges dorés me donnent l'idée du surnom de la voiture qui conservera l'acronyme MG: ce sera Malachite-Gold. ' (With the paint job finished, the reassembly of the mechanics and accessories could begin. The interior would be done in beige: leather seats, headrest and armrest, vinyl trim and a thick carpet in a darker shade of beige on the floor. The new mohair hood would have a beige lining. The combination of mallard green and golden beige gave me an idea for the car's name, retaining the initials MG. I would call her Malachite Gold.)

'Le 1 er mars 2003, j'effectue les premiers tours de roues dans les environ du garage. Il reste quelques finitions à faire, mais le 18 mars, le carrossier la fait passer en conformité sans problème. Il faut maintenant attendre les papiers officiels qui permettront de l'immatriculer. Cela va prendre deux mois! Avec entre-temps une multitude de coups de téléphone, de lettres recommandées et de visites auprès des autorités. Le 15 mai, enfin, j'obtiens mes plaques et je peux faire assurer la voiture.' (On 1 March 2003, I took my first drive around the garage yard, with some details still to finish. On 18 March, we received the compliance certificate. No problem, but the official papers to register the car would take two months with, in the meantime, a multitude of phone calls, registered letters and visits to the authorities. On 15 May finally, I had my plates and I could insure the car.)

'L'été 2003, c'est la canicule sur toute l'Europe. On ne pouvait pas imaginer meilleures conditions pour rouler en décapotable. Les premiers déplacements sont assez limités, car les petites pannes sont assez nombreuses dans ces premiers kilomètres. À partir de 2004, on effectue quelques voyages (Normandie, Languedoc, Luxembourg) et on participe à des rassemblements un peu partout en Belgique'. (The summer of 2003 was a heatwave across Europe. There could be no better weather for riding in a convertible. The early trips were rather limited, because little hiccups kept happening before we'd got very far, but from 2004 we made some long journeys (Normandy, Languedoc and Luxemburg) and we joined in with rallies across Belgium.)

'Quelques longs voyages nous tentent encore (Royaume-Uni ou Autriche par exemple), mais, personnellement, le plus délassant c'est l'utilisation de Malachite-Gold au quotidien. N'étant pas immatriculée en catégorie 'ancêtre', mais avec une plaque normale, je peux l'utiliser pour aller au travail ou pour me rendre à des réunions et rendez-vous divers, pourvu que le temps le permette.' (We plan some more long trips (in United Kingdom or Austria for example), but personally, I'm just as happy and relaxed in Malachite Gold doing ordinary daily driving. Not being registered in the veteran category, but with a normal plate, I can go to work in her, or to meetings and various appointments, weather permitting.)

'Mes étudiants l'ont repérée et ont même pastiché une petite vidéo lors d'une de leur fête annuelle. Un collègue a qui je l'ai fait essayer n'a pas résisté à ses charmes, et s'est empressé d'acheter et de faire rénover une très belle MGA 1600.' (My students, taking note of my car, made a comic video for one of their annual parties. A colleague, whom I invited to try the MG, could not resist her charms and immediately went out and bought a beautiful MGA 1600 for restoration.)

'Sur la route, les réactions sont diverses. Celles des enfants sont toujours amusantes: "Regarde Maman, la drôle de petite voiture!" "Monsieur, elle roule vraiment ta voiture?" Mais beaucoup de Belges moyens vivent pour leur voiture et n'admettent pas que l'on remette en cause leur hiérarchie de valeurs: SUV, 4x4, grandes routières allemandes, diesel et en couleur gris-casserole de préférence. (On the road, I get various reactions. Those from children are always humorous: "Mummy, look at the funny little car". "Please sir, does your car actually go?" But your average Belgians love their cars and don't see any possibilities beyond their SUVs, four by fours and large German saloons, preferably diesel and in battleship grey.)

'Cela se traduit parfois par des comportements peu élégants sur la route. Tel conducteur d'âge mûr au volant d'une grosse BMW tenant à tout prix à démarrer le premier au feu rouge, tel jeune 'Jacky' prenant tous les risques pour dépasser au volant de sa Seat pseudo-tunée hurlant de la musique techno par ses fenêtres ouvertes. Mais le regard admiratif de leur compagne depuis le siège passager me fait prendre tout cela avec le sourire.' (This sometimes leads to rude behaviour on the road. There's the mature driver in the big BMW, desperate to be away first at the lights, or the boy racer taking any risk to overtake in his souped-up Seat screaming techno music from its open windows. But the admiring glance of his girlfriend from the passenger seat makes me take it all with a smile.)

'Quand, on contraire, on perçoit un signe de sympathie ou que l'on croise une autre ancienne sur la route avec un appel de phares, on al'étonnante mais agréable sensation de ne pas avoir perdu sa journée.' (On the other hand, when you get a friendly wave or when you pass another classic car with a flash of the headlights, it kind of makes your day.)

'Je regard des centaines de sites de clubs, de vendeurs, d'amateurs, d'entreprises automobile et évidemment dans un anglais technique qui est loin du 'basic English' utilisé professionnellement. Si les sites anglo-saxons consacrés aux MG sont nombreux, je me suis dit que la mise à disposition sur le Web de cette documentation en français – assortie d'un petit glossaire – pourrait sans doute aider d'autres enthousiastes francophones.' (I looked at the hundreds of websites of clubs, dealers, enthusiasts, and for automotive parts and tools, and of course all is in English, and not just the basic English we use at work. With so many English language sites devoted to MG, I thought that publishing on the web in French – together with a short glossary – might help other French-speaking fans.)

'En outre, les ressources iconographiques sont innombrables (dessins techniques, humoristiques et artistiques, catalogues, affiches publicitaires, photos prises lors

Regarde Maman, la drôle de petite voiture. Monsieur, elle roule vraiment?

de salons et de compétition). Comme je m'étais mis aussi à relever les apparitions de MG dans ma collection de bandes dessinées et dans mes quelques vidéos, je disposais d'un matériel susceptible d'alimenter un site Web un peu original.' (In addition, graphic resources are endless (technical, humorous and artistic drawings, catalogues, posters, photos taken during shows and competitions). As I also had pictures of MGs in my collection of comics and in various videos, I felt I had enough material for a quite novel website.)

'Mis en ligne en 2004, il a connu un petit succès et s'est enrichi au fil des années, en particulier par une collection assez exhaustive de fiches sur tous les modèles de la marque MG (jusqu'en 1981 mais y compris les prototypes et les MG spéciales), et par des photos prises lors de quelques évènements belges marquants, en particulier à Francorchamps.' (We went on line in 2004 and we've had fair success and growth over the years, including a near-comprehensive collection of fact sheets on all the models of the MG marque until 1981, with prototypes and MG specials, and pictures taken at some notable events in Belgium, particularly in Francorchamps.)

'Il y a aussi bien sûr une rubrique consacrée à Malachite-Gold, sa rénovation et ses voyages, mais aussi une rubrique dédiée aux exploits de Stirling Moss sur MGB, aimablement cautionnée – et je n'en suis pas peu fier – par Sir Stirling lui-même. La plus belle page Web du site est pourtant, selon moi, celle du livre d'or. Alors, si vous avez l'occasion, ne vous privez pas.' (As you might expect, there are pages dedicated to Malachite Gold's renovation and travels, but we also have a page devoted to the exploits of Stirling Moss in the MGB, kindly supported – I'm proud to say – by Sir Stirling himself. Even so, the best page on the site in my view is the guestbook. So if you have the opportunity, don't miss it.)

Merci beaucoup. C'est ici. http://www.geomatique-liege.be/MGJP/index.htm

---

On running out of petrol

'I was driving in the British Isles in 1938, and came one day to a sudden, coughing stop in a far and lonely section of Scotland. The car had run out of gas in the wilderness. This car's gasoline guage had a trick of mounting toward 'Full' instead of sinking toward 'Empty' when the tank was running low, one of the many examples of pure cussedness of which it was capable. There I was, miles from any village, with not even a farmhouse in sight. On my left was a thick wood, out of which the figure of a man suddenly appeared. He asked me what the matter was and I said I had run out of petrol. 'It just happens,' he told me, 'That I have a can of petrol.' With that, he went back into the woods, and came out again with a five-gallon can of gasoline. He put it in the tank for me, I thanked him, paid for it, and drove on.

Once when I was telling this true but admittedly remarkable story, at a party in New York, a bright-eyed young woman exclaimed, 'But when the man emerged from the lonely woods, miles away from any village, far from the nearest farmhouse, carrying a five-gallon can of gasoline, why didn't you ask him how he happened to be there with it?'. I lighted a cigarette. 'Madam,' I said, 'I was afraid he would vanish.' She gave a small laugh and moved away from me.'

(*Recollections of the Gas Buggy*, James Thurber.)

CHAPTER EIGHTEEN

On Cutting the Pumpkin

'I think the car is getting noiser,' said Dorothy Bremer. Her husband, Dick, driving the TC, had spent some time before setting out on this trip, installing a reconditioned Austin differential, and he had been hoping that the gear noise he could hear was in his worried mind and not in reality. He pulled over.

They were not in a good spot for a car problem, about twenty miles north of Munising in Michigan's Upper Peninsula. The citizens of Munising and Alger County pride themselves on their scenic attractions for wilderness explorers, and define a wilderness as a place where people visit but do not remain. This definition suited the Bremers, on their way from Ohio in a small convoy of MG-ers to a Gathering of the Faithful in Duluth, Minnesota, but remaining seemed a clear possibility to Dick as he got out of the car.

He believed he had solved his trouble with oil leaking from the axles by redoing the seals, and he'd fitted a pressure relief device on the banjo (axle housing) because the Austin diff had hypoid gears which created pressure. These measures had not worked. He suspected that he might have fried the rear end, with oil leaking much faster than he'd thought.

Hindsight, as we know, is a wonderful thing, and with its aid we can say that Dick should have poured any kind of oil into the diff and driven slowly to the next town, about twenty five miles distant. Instead, what he did was hitch his car to the TF of his Ohio friend Jim, without adding any oil, and the journey finished the job of trashing the rear end.

After a hairy tow of an hour, along a hilly, curving road, constantly riding the brakes to keep tension on the rope, they reached Harvey, Marquette County, population 1,300. They went by a garage, a basic sort of a place to say the least, with junked cars and car junk piled up in the yard. A fellow walked out of the workshop, spotted them and waved them in, but they were already past and needed to turn around. This was considered a worthwhile thing to do as they felt they were likely to encounter the more understanding type of motor man, rather than one steeped in official regulations and procedures. They pulled into a side street, broke the tow strap by winding it around the front axle, tied it back together, and set off to meet the proprietor of the messiest workshop either had ever seen. Whatever the first impressions, the fellow was a no-nonsense, can-do kind of guy and he was glad to let them use his shop and tools.

His two hoists were circa 1930 but worked perfectly. With the TC in the air, Dick hesitated before moving under it. He asked the man – let's call him Noggin – if the hoist had safety stops that needed to be set. Noggin said: 'You from OSHA or what?'

For the benefit of those unfamiliar with American life, OSHA is the Occupational, Safety and Health Administration, an organisation that lives well up to its name, and the abrupt response defined Noggin as a true Youper, that is, one who exhibits

I'm sure your dear Mama will love it, sir. Congratulations.

And this is what it's all about.

Taking the car back home to Médoc.

the characteristics of rural life in remote areas such as the Upper Pensinsula (a UP-er becomes a Youper, geddit?). In other parts of the world we also have rural life in remote areas and our equivalents of Youpers, and in Europe we now have the EU-OSHA, responsible for regulating the height of tractor seats, the number of persons required to change a public light bulb, the correct distance between the tines of garden forks, and many other important matters.

In no time, Jim and Dick had the banjo unbolted and had the pumpkin (the part of the diff that bolts into the axle housing) on the bench, gently pushing aside the debris of centuries. What they had suspected was correct. The diff had run dry and was ruined. In the very centre of Hicksville without the ville, there surely would be sufficient difficulty in finding a way to get the car home, without even thinking about fixing it.

Noggin said that he had recently been out to a junk yard where he'd seen a couple of sporty looking old cars. Maybe it would be worth a drive to see if they might be of any use. With nothing to lose but some time, and with Noggin's directions, Dick and Jim went forth. Deep in the woods on a remote back road, half an hour later they discovered the yard and were made welcome.

Walking through rows of bodies lying in the weeds, they spotted what looked like a Sprite or a Midget sitting on top of a wreck resembling a Mustang convertible. It was doubtful whether the rear end would fit the TC but that didn't matter anyway because someone had already removed the rear axle. Scanning further for unconsidered trifles, Jim spotted something that could once have been sort of small and British. 'Isn't that a Morris Traveller over there, in the briar patch?' he asked.

This was a golden discovery. Such a car might well have a rear end like the one in the TC. They hurried back to the shop and asked the man if he could tip the car up so they could see what was what, and he said sure and got his old wrecker out. With the car over on its side, they could confirm their delight, which would cost them only $75. Their saviour dragged a cutting torch out of the back of the wrecker and started to cut the pumpkin out of the car. The taped acetylene hose caught fire. After getting that extinguished, he cut the axle tube and the oil in the axle caught fire. The saviour in question apologised, saying the owner wasn't there and he was just filling in, but the firefighters won and, after letting the oil drain away, finished removing the centre part of the rear axle. Pumpkin off; perfect condition.

A later BMC pumpkin would not fit into a TC banjo without modification, so they would have to use the case from the Austin pumpkin Dick had modified. The tolerances stamped on the two cases revealed that there was only two thousandths of an inch difference. Noggin and Jim sagely agreed that there would be no problem in doing the case swap, and the gear ratio was the same as the original TC.

While Jim was dismantling the Morris pumpkin, Dick took on the cleaning of the old case. He asked Noggin if he had a parts cleaner somewhere. He had an air hose, a spray gun and a can of gasoline. Dick got to work and noticed, out of the corner of his eye, Jim's passenger in the TF, a chain smoker called Peter, sauntering out of the shop to light up.

That scene at the gas station from Hitchcock's *The Birds* played instantly across Dick's brain. He dropped the air hose and shouted at Peter to stop, but too late. Luckily, the deadly conflagration did not manifest, and the smoker was encouraged to indulge his habit elsewhere.

The Miracle of Marquette concluded happily. They paid Noggin $100 for the use of his shop, his expertise and local knowledge, and were in Duluth by nine that evening.

CHAPTER NINETEEN

The Law of Unintended Consequences Explained

Xavier Bouchenot's parents, like so many, were largely unaware of the Law of Unintended Consequences. This law is every bit as important as $E = MC^2$, maybe more so, and it states:

'Every action meant to influence matters may or may not have the desired result but will, regardless of that, have at least one unimagined outcome and possibly several.'

The action in this case was by Madame Bouchenot. She gave little Xavier, aged nine, a plastic model kit, the desired result being a few hours of quiet and constructive activity. It worked. He built the model, and it was an MG TC, a car unseen by the boy up to that point, growing up in the Médoc where, as we know, the main concern in life is red wine. Xavier may have made his parents smile while brumm-brumming his model car across the carpet (or whatever the French is for brumm-brumm), but the unintended consequence was a new and insistent craving to move up from model to real thing.

The means was in the garage, a Peugeot 201 from 1929, the first year of manufacture, with van body and trade proclaimed along the side as belonging to the local *boulangerie*. It was almost falling to pieces but the boy Xavier decided he would learn and do everything necessary to get that car back on the road, and he did. He was driving it one day when a Dutch tourist saw him, and it, and wanted to buy. Xavier was not keen on a deal, but the Dutchman returned the next year, and the next, by which time Xavier was eighteen. He needed money to pay for official driving lessons, his test and his licence, matters which had somehow been neglected until then, and so he sold the car.

Fast forward to 2005 and Xavier was past his fortieth birthday, the point in his life when he had decided to award himself the TC of his fancy, fulfilling an ambition of more than thirty years. In between he'd had a 1961 frog-eye Sprite and several BMW motorbikes, but now he could be observed looking in the window of an MG mecca, the showrooms of Brown and Gammons Ltd on Baldock high street, once the Great North Road before the bypass was built. He was here to look, not at a TC but at a TB, registered ETD 181, built in July 1939. The original owner is not known (registration indicates the Lancashire area), but it was in the hands of C P Roderick of 4 Chester Square, London SW1 in 1968. It seems to have been off the road for a while after that, being restored, and C J Charles bought it from a garage on the A4 near Reading, possibly took it to the 1975 MG Jubilee gathering, and he sold it in 1990 to Ron Gammons, who had little to do apart from general maintenance.

Into each life, some rain must fall, but I'm
still not putting the roof up.

Xavier looking cool on the racetrack. His number plate appears to have been hit by a low-flying
bumble bee.

The chateaux of France have a certain style about them. It makes sense for anyone visiting to do so likewise in style and, really, you can't beat an MG for that.

In 1970 Ron Benson was an engineering apprentice at Dorman Long, Thornaby, the firm that built Sydney Harbour bridge and, more famously, the bridge over the Esk at Ruswarp. The Bensons's neighbour had a TA in which he commuted from Stokesley to London by the week, and Ron thought it 'a great looking car' so, when he came to buy a first car of his own, a 1939 TB seemed the obvious choice.

He rebuilt it, finishing with a paint job in coach enamel applied by brush, and went to work in it every day. At last it began to protest in so many small ways that Ron decided to solve all the problems in one big hit, and embarked on a second rebuild.

Here she is, going up the Rosedale Chimney Bank in 2009, the road between Rosedale Abbey and Hutton-le-Hole, often used for hill climbs. Coming up from the valley floor of the Northdale Beck, which runs into the River Seven, in parts it inclines to one in three, a gradient steep enough to defeat many a motor but not Ron's TB.

Xavier has made some epic voyages in his TB. One memorable journey was from Versailles to Bordeaux, 580 kilometres (360 miles) in one night, open top, mostly at a steady 55–65mph, which was 3800–4200 rpm in fourth, but the most magnificent unimagined outcome was a week's holiday in Germany for Madame Bouchenot, the mother who gave her little boy that plastic model kit all those years before. Xavier took her in the TB on a round trip of 3000 kilometres (1,860 miles) with never a problem.

You might think, after easy success in such trials, there must be a catch somewhere, and you would be right. It came in the form of a Parisian bus, in the Place de la Porte Maillot, on a grey day – 15 August 2007, in fact. Xavier had had a new hood fitted, although he very rarely used the old one, and had been instructed to keep the hood up for two weeks. The bus driver who overtook him looked down on a tiny car with a cloth roof and obviously expected such a vehicle to give way as they turned into a corner. Said bus driver would not have known that the combination of right-hand drive and unaccustomed hood rendered Xavier unable to see the great behemoth looming over him and, inevitably, crushing his little car with a crack and a bang. The repairs are going to take a long while.

Many people's top cat, the TC makes her point on an American driveway with lesser vehicles beyond.

In 1929, the year this car was made, Imperial Airways would have flown you from Croydon to various European destinations in an Armstrong Whitworth Argosy, a three engined biplane taking 18 passengers and a crew of two, plus a steward to serve you lunch. Only seven of these aircraft were built; none remain, obviously, and neither do any other similar machines. Should you want to travel in Europe in 1929 style today, the suggestion is a car like this, an MG 18/80.

Is this your car, signore? That's a very impressive array of instruments. Have you got one that tells you how fast you're going?

CHAPTER TWENTY

Aeroplanes? Who Needs 'Em?

The Law of Unintended Consequences appears elsewhere in this book, in several places in fact, and its effects are amply demonstrated in the case of the MG and Mr and Mrs John and Janet Day.

John's mother died and left him some money. He thought long and hard about what he and Janet might spend it on, in particular trying to keep in mind what would have been his mother's preferences in the matter. He knew that at the bottom of any list his mother might have drawn up would have been 'an old car', if such a thing had even managed to get on the list, but he knew also that his mum would have wanted him to be happy, so he decided to buy an old car.

He set out looking for a four-seater N type Magnette, for touring, but then another tourer came on the market, WL 7196, a six cylinder, two and a half litre classic of classics, vintage of vintages, one of the very few living examples of the first proper MG, the 18/80 Tourer. As soon as John saw it, he forgot all about N types. This, he felt, had been built especially for him – before he was born, admittedly, but the power, rarity and sheer presence of the car hit him right where Cupid aims his arrows.

He found that the restoration of his 1929 car had been perfect in many ways, especially cosmetically, but alas not so mechanically. 'Show not go' is the technical term, and she broke down nearly every time John and Janet tried to go out for a drive. Most of the problems were minor or, if major, still fixable at the roadside. The only time the RAC had to be called was when the main drive shaft in the torque tube sheared.

John is a retired aeronautical engineer, a man of the jet age, giving him a set of skills not entirely suited to vintage mechanics but the aptitude, abilities and general knowledge were all there. Over the years, he rebuilt the moving parts with 'going' as top priority – by which he meant going on modern roads for long distances.

She cost John £30,000 in 1996. Today, he could get £75,000, so that's something mother could be pleased about, but the real point, the unintended consequence, is the change the car has made in the Days' lives.

John had the car's mechanics more or less sorted by the year 2000, so it seemed like a good idea to embark on a trip of 2,000 miles. They went for a holiday in the Loire, then drove across France and Belgium into Holland, to the MGCC European Event of the Year at Arnhem. A few small electrical difficulties were all that impeded their progress, easily fixed by an aero engineer, and by the time they got home they'd done the two thousand.

To be carried most of the way to Gabicce Mare on the Italian Adriatic coast, and all the way back, was not entirely the plan in 2001. They drove to 's-Hertogenbosch, AKA Den Bosch, where there is a terminal for the motorail that could take them overnight to Bologna, and they could motor in self-propelled fashion the rest of the way. Italian MG fans were highly appreciative of a car that most had only seen in a picture before, but appreciation turned to grief when six days of mountainous eventing proved too much and, on the last day, they broke a half shaft. With no spare and no possibility of getting one, they did what they had to do: called the RAC.

For those who have not used RAC Recovery overseas, this is what happens. A local firm picks up your car and looks after it until an opportunity crops up for a suitable return journey, usually in a covered British transporter that has brought cars out and would otherwise go back empty. The Days can surely claim the record for RAC Recovery of 1929 MGs: 1,100 miles from mid-Italy to Bedford.

Annual continental holidays with an MG theme became the norm. Some were not so ambitious, just a drive to the European Event in Belgium and a tour of northern France in the company of three more modern MGs (Well, they would have to be, wouldn't they? Since the 18/80 was the original MG that wasn't a Morris, all other MGs are more modern.)

There was Viborg in Denmark; ferry to the Hook, 750 miles each way, no problems at all with the car. Another time, twenty owners of vintage MGs took over a small chateau near Tours, on the Loire, for a week of convivial MG-ing. The locals marvelled at the cars and were most welcoming, and far too polite to complain about stains left by a few incontinent vehicles on their immaculate block-paved car parks.

Another vintage outing in Brittany in May 2005 was followed by the Event of the Year in Holland, Clermont Ferrand in 2006, Speyer in Germany 2007, and the most testing of all, Zug in Switzerland, 2008. This Event celebrated sixty years of the Swiss MG Car Club and John, as chairman of the UK mother club, made a speech at the gala dinner with representatives of thirteen European nations present. That was the easy bit. A week's rally in the Alps, in the middle of a 2,000 mile round trip, would test any old car but, as we already know, John's 18/80 is not any old car. She managed the spectacular but forbidding Klausen Pass with no bother, 136 bends climbing 3,700 feet to the summit at well over six thousand feet, and no recourse had to be made this time to that other automobile club.

The 2009 event was in Norway, which was appealing, but they settled an another holiday in the Loire instead, and looked forward to Gabbice Mare again in 2010.

In an average year, John and Janet will do 5,000 miles in that car. Altogether, from birth as it were, she's done 400,000. In John's own words, 'she's as reliable as a modern car. Well, nearly. She's a beautiful car, comfortable for long distances, attracts a lot of attention because she's so rare, and I enjoy the challenge of driving a grand old car in the way Cecil Kember intended, over eighty years after it was made. That doesn't usually include top-speeding at 80mph, although she'll do it. I cruise at 60 on the motorways, keeping a bit in reserve for passing lorries. No need to over-stress the old lady.'

The car in front is John Day's 18/80. The car behind is another one, the fabric bodied saloon version, belonging to MGCC stalwart Doug Harris.

A fine day in Germany, near Oldenburg, on the way to Denmark for the Event of the Year. Janet looks like she wants to get a move on, but John can never have enough photographs.

Three classics and a man who surely cannot be doing what it looks like.

Nightmare on Bridge Street

Sometime in the 1970s, a design engineer had the idea of putting a computer in a car. At that instant, an entire breed was sentenced to professional decline and eventual extinction.

We can expect people who mend cars commercially to have disappeared from the western world by about 2020 AD. Then, there will remain only a few isolated individuals, dedicated enthusiasts, among whom will reside the last shreds of knowledge about how to repair cars such as MGs, rather than psychoanalyse them and reconstitute them with plug-in components. If he hasn't retired by then, one of those individuals will be Ralph Harrison (pronounced Raarf in the Westmorland way), whose premises on Bridge Street, Appleby-in-Westmorland, Cumbria, UK, are exactly the same as they and many others were in the Age of the Grease Nipple.

Inside a dark cavern with a large and deep rectangular hole in the floor, burns a stove fuelled by sump waste. Parked against one wall you will see some motorcycles (BSA C15, Ariel Square Four, Triumph Tiger Cub, Norton Dominator). On other walls hang the bonnet and wheels of a Riley Elf, a TC radiator grille, a number of half-worn tyres and several wiring harnesses on a hook.

To the left is a door through to the shop which stocks parts and lubricants. If you have an account, Ralph writes your purchases on the blotter. It is not known how this data is captured from myriad other similar scratchings on the old and tattered blotting paper and transferred to your bill in six months' time.

In the chaotic area designated 'office', there is a picture of a Jowett Javelin, some horrible items to do with making tea, and a girlie calendar for 1972 provided by RW Grimbagg & Sons (Abrasives) Ltd.

The man himself, a small, jolly, roundish sort of a chap, in a dark blue overall, is often to be found sitting on a bench with a couple of like minds. They might well be sharing a lamb jalfraisi with prawn biriani, part-payment for a job Ralph did last year on the Mini Moke owned by the daughter of a local restaurateur.

If there is something wrong with your car, and it's a proper car, such as an MG, Ralph will ratch about and find something with which to fix it. Genial, always pleasant, always and ever helpful, the Ralphs of this world are, like common sense, not as common as they used to be. If you want to find another in the UK, you will need to go to a small country town (non-commutable) or the back streets of a poor area of the city, possibly under a railway viaduct. Look for a rusty sign saying 'National Benzole' or 'Pratt's Motor Spirit' and there, in a dark cavern with a rectangular hole in the floor…

CHAPTER TWENTY ONE

Everyone has Life-Defining Moments

You see someone across a crowded room and, thirty years later, you're still talking. You have your first beer; you don't like it but you persevere and, abracadabra, you do like it. You see a certain type of car go past and, yes, well, we all know that story.

Or, being an MG owner already, you happen to click on a German website (www. mgcc.de, in fact) which offers a list of memorabilia several kilometres in length, and you spot the interesting information that there is a postage stamp with a picture of your car on it. You go, for the first time in your existence, into a stamp collecting shop and ask about this stamp. To your utter amazement and before your very eyes, the old fellow behind the counter does not look at you as if you are bonkers, but instead searches briefly in his stock and finds it, a used 70 dinar stamp issued by the Yugoslavian postal authority to commemorate a 1953 car rally, with a drawing of a Y-type on it, supposedly hurtling through the mountain snow.

For an all-in price of very little, the stamp man then adds a 300 franc 1996 Congo Republic with an MGA on it, and an eight peso 1984 Guinea-Bissau showing a 1932 J2 Midget. Very probably, unless you are Portuguese, you don't know much about Guinea-Bissau.

You could, if you were the curious type, find out fairly easily that the Republic of Guinea-Bissau, formerly Portuguese Guinea, AKA the Slave Coast, on the western side of Africa, is a very small and very poor country with one of the lowest figures for wealth production in the world, plagued throughout its short independent history by coups, assassinations and civil wars. If its stamps were to be truly representative, they would show fish and cashew nuts. Certainly we can be sure that hardly any of the 1,700,000 population have ever seen a real MG.

These were matters which did not, at the time, grip the subject of this particular life-changing moment. No, he was suddenly in thrall to an urge familiar to many MG owners: to collect MG-related objects. The task Willem van der Veer, of Ermelo, Holland, set himself was to find an example of every stamp ever issued that had an MG on it. There was a slight worry, of course. Stamp collecting, like train spotting and rug making, is not a hobby widely considered appropriate for the sort of chap whose image otherwise centres around sporty vehicles. This did not bother Willem. His stamps were not of that stamp. His stamps were going to have MGs on them, so that was all right.

His first investigations revealed treasure that stretched credence. With no difficulty at all, he soon found well over forty of these stamps, and some from the most obscure countries. Be honest, reader. Have you ever heard of Batum, Nagaland, or Komi? The Republic of Komi, part of the Russian Federation, consists almost entirely of lakes, forests, rivers and swamps and lies to the west of the Urals. The

It's a family thing, this stamp collecting.

national sport is bandy, a sort of cross between ice hockey and soccer, very good for the frozen lakes that they have a lot of the time. When we say 'they', we mean about one million people in a country roughly two thirds the size of France.

Nagaland? You've heard of Assam and Burma. Well, it's near there. Why Batum should have stamps isn't clear, much less why any of them should depict an M-type. It's a city, actually Batumi, capital of the Republic of Adjara, which you've also never heard of, on the Black Sea next to Georgia. Abkhazia, again formerly USSR and disputedly part of Georgia, is another of Willem's MG-stamp countries, as is Udmertia, central Russia.

In none of these places would you walk down the street expecting to see any kind of MG. The Yugoslavians did have a link, in that the car on the stamp did compete in their Jugoslovenski Alpski Rallye, but normally the streets of Dubrovnik and Belgrade would not have offered many sightings in 1953 or any other time. In countries where MGs were more commonplace, those countries have little or nothing in common with the Udmert Republic. So why, is the question.

The clue is perhaps in the 1977 Equatorial Guinea 50 ekuele. It shows the profile of a P-type Airline Coupé and describes it as a 1934 Panhard and Levassor. The reason for putting this design on the stamp is therefore not through MG high regard; it can only be appreciation of sheer beauty.

We cannot know how many committee meetings, or how large were the committees, that met to discuss proposals for the new Kyrgyzstan twenty som stamp for the year 2000. We can never be privy to the agonies of the designers, working till midnight to satisfy the demands of unreasonable Kyrgyzstani postal officials. We can only understand the relief those designers must have felt when someone suggested this picture, this one here, of a car. They didn't know it was a K3 but they knew the committee would love it, and they were right.

Willem's researches have now revealed that there are at least sixty four stamps in the world with MGs, and at the latest count he has sixty of them. Why, he asks, is it that five of them show M-types? Why is the Yugoslavian Y the only saloon among all of them? What do the islands of Nevis, St Vincent and Tuvalu have in common, that they show MGs on their stamps?

The answer to the last question is easy. Those postal authorities, and about sixty others worldwide, issue stamps mainly for collectors to buy, with posting the secondary consideration, and they use the American Inter-Governmental Philatelic Corporation (www.igpc.net) to produce them. This company began its upward ascent in 1957, when the British colony of Gold Coast became the independent Ghana and found it didn't know quite what to do about its postal system. It outsourced stamp origination and IGPC has never looked back. Now it claims almost half of the world's new stamp designs. There may be something odd about collecting things that are deliberately manufactured to be collected, but there would not be so many MG stamps otherwise.

Willem has almost reached the point of a complete collection, so what is left for him? Every stamp can be researched, he says. For example, did Walt Disney own an MGA, as he is pictured with one on the $1 2004 stamp from Timor? What are Micky and Minnie Mouse doing, sitting in a 1956 blue MGA in the middle of a golf course, courtesy of a $3

Maybe these cars are still around. Who owns them? The white TC was originally a right-hand drive going in the other direction.

stamp from Redonda? Since you ask, Redonda is a large rock in the Leeward Islands with no golf and no post office, which is hardly surprising as it has no inhabitants either, apart from a squillion seabirds and a few wild goats. And, having decided to incorporate the said Mice and an MGA into the picture, who then thought of adding a mad golfer who looks like Colonel Sanders on holiday from his Kentucky chicken fryer?

Willem wondered if it was an NA or an NB Magnette on the Cambodian 4500 riel, year 2000, although now he knows it must be an A because the B had a slatted radiator grille, except the A had suicide doors and the Cambodian N has front-hinged doors and a lower scuttle so it must be a B. Final answer. And then he noticed through his magnifying glass (yes, he has become a stamp collector) that the Yugoslavian Y has its rear side window missing.

An extra dimension to the research comes with finding the current owners of the cars depicted on the stamps. For example, not sure of the differences between a PA and a PB as shown on the stamps from Komi, Willem contacted Brian Kelly of Kansas and the Triple-M Register (part of the MG Car Club, the three Ms representing Midget, Magna and Magnette). Both cars were alive and well and on the register. Brian pointed out that the PA has a honeycombed grille while the PB has the famous MG slatted one, and the PB owner ended up getting a set of Komi stamps for his Christmas box.

Still to be discovered are the owners of: white TC with registration number MG 5225, Republic of Komi; green J2, registration MG 3024, Rwanda; red TC, registration 883, Guernsey; K3, JB 1475, Kyrgyzstan; red M-type, MG 527, Batum. If anyone has any information about these cars, please contact Willem via his website www. mgstamps.shorturl.com

So how did it all start? Willem's parents were MG-ers. They took him, aged six, and his brother to the annual MG meeting at Silverstone where those two small boys were deeply impressed with the racing. Willem still has a clear picture in his mind, some 40 years on, of being allowed to sit in an NE in the pits, but the most brilliant memory is of a golden YA, driven by Frank Vautier, cornering almost on two wheels. It was then he decided that, one day, he had to have a YA.

The years passed. Willem's unfulfilled love was renewed on the rare occasions he chanced to see a Y, but there never was one for sale so he bought his father's MGB Tourer. Countless MG meetings in Holland and elsewhere only solidified his conviction that he should give up hope of ever owning a Y. Then, in the May 2003 issue of the Dutch MGCC magazine, there was one advertised, original registration NKJ 443 (therefore from Kent).

An elderly enthusiast had been 'kindly asked' by his wife to reduce his collection of old cars and motorcycles. Willem told himself that, as he had never even sat in a Y, his high regard for the model was but fantasy. The many years' distance of Silverstone and Frank Vautier had lent enchantment to the view. Being closely confronted by the real thing, he would certainly be disappointed. So, with self-delusion turned up to 'full', he went, he saw, he fell.

The bodywork had several bodged repairs that Willem preferred not to notice, and he knew he was in for a lifetime of tinkering and caring but, with its original interior and basically sound mechanics, he was also in for many happy family trips across Europe, every one much more of a memorable adventure than could be possible in a modern car.

CHAPTER TWENTY TWO

A Piece of Plywood Makes
all the Difference

When Jack Hardy first saw the PA, he noted several non-standard modifications, one of which turned out to be the make or break. The rear seat had been replaced by a ¾-inch thick piece of plywood that had a small trap-door for getting at the battery. There were homemade cushions instead of the rear bucket seats and a bench-type seat back. To the casual observer, the PA looked like the two-seat version. Jack's problem was that the current owner, F S Carli, had a buyer for it as a two-seater. Ah but, this buyer didn't want it if it was a four-seater. Jack had the textbooks with him, convinced Mr Carli that it was really the four-seat model, and agreed a price.

This was in June 1994. For various reasons, restoration couldn't start until the following spring so Jack did some research, learning that the car was bought new on April 27 1935 by G Gallowhur from University Motors, the London dealership that served MG for many a year but is no longer in business (there are several firms by that name in the USA, some indeed specialising in MGs).

Mr Gallowhur had the car for less than a year; it went in March 1936 to R G Cooper of Cardiff. The move across the Atlantic came in 1939, when Randall Keator of Rumson, New Jersey, imported it and kept it for ten years. His successor was Skitch Henderson of New York, and his were Mr and Mrs D D and G Johnston, who travelled the world and took the car with them.

THE CUNARD STEAM-SHIP COMPANY LIMITED.

AUTO SHIPMENT No.

OWNER'S NAME Mr. G. L. Johnston

TYPE CAR —OPEN/CLOSED— MAKE M-G.

SHIPPED PER Queen Elizabeth DATE 8/5/68

FROM Southampton TO New York

REMARKS

G85/768

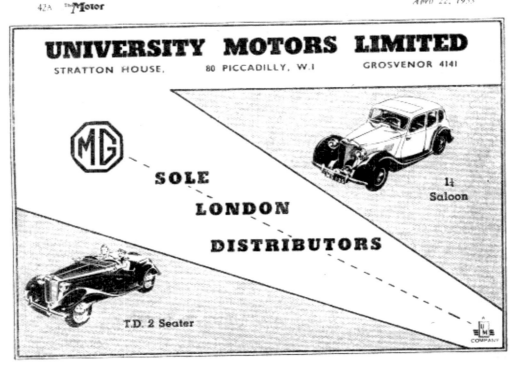

42A   The Motor   April 22, 1953

UNIVERSITY MOTORS LIMITED

STRATTON HOUSE,   80 PICCADILLY, W.I   GROSVENOR 4141

MG

SOLE

LONDON

DISTRIBUTORS

1¼ Saloon

T.D. 2 Seater

That was from 1960 to 1989, when F S Carli took it down to Nevada City and that's where it was when Jack and Sherri Hardy, of Monrovia discovered PA 1875 in less than perfect order.

In March 1995 Jack started his restoration work; the first job obviously being to disassemble the car completely, then clean and paint the chassis frame so he could begin putting it back together. During the disassembly he discovered that all the components with serial numbers matched the factory delivery sheet. Such originality was very welcome, and inspirational towards keeping it that way.

Even so, there were signs that others had not been so minded. Carburettors were down-draught Zeniths of less than one inch on a home-made manifold, while the original manifold, enlarged to 1½ inch, was still available because it had come to Jack with the car. He bought a pair of used 1½-inch SUs (HV-2) and fitted them.

Also non-standard were the dashboard and some of the instruments. Jack purchased correct PA temperature gauges, odometer and switches, and had the original instruments and controls restored by Vintage Restorations. He needed a replacement dashboard, so he thought he might as well make two, with half-inch birch aircraft plywood and sequoia burl veneer. He traded the extra dashboard plus a wheel for a pair of bucket seats.

Now Jack did some non-standard designing himself. As described already, there was no back seat so he decided to leave it that way, giving extra storage space, replacing the old work with new plywood. He had a new hood made, copied from the one that came with the car and replaced the worst of the chrome. Leaving some chrome items showing wear seemed to him to add character, as a reference to all the use that had gone before.

The engine was rebuilt with all new internal components (cylinder bores were found very useable at 60.5mm, PB size (0.020 over). One bore had been sleeved and was cracked; it was re-sleeved and bored to match the others.

Modern oil seals front, rear and in the vertical drive for the camshaft were installed. All the engine machine work, valves, re-sleeving/boring, modifications for seals and balancing was done by a local machinist. The flywheel was lightened by a fellow Vintage MG club member, to early factory dimensions.

The transmission's gears looked OK, showing little wear, so only the bearings were replaced. A bearing was put in the front of the transmission to act as an oil seal.

The differential had a modified (sawn off) pinion gear and was a non-standard ratio. The CWP and bearings were replaced with a standard set. The rear axle housing was straightened from its curved form. Both axles and hubs were replaced; the old hubs were loose on the axles. New sealed bearings were installed along with new bearing carriers.

The rear springs were MGTA or something near that and one was shorter than the other as a result of having an eye re-rolled. New ones were fitted.

The Bishop Cam steering gear was badly worn in its bearing races, so the worm, peg and bearing were replaced with new components. Another VMG club member installed the worm to its shaft and fitted needle bearings and lip seal on the sector

PA1875 sometime between 1939 and 1949, with owner Randall Keator, New Jersey.

Tub at Carli's

shaft. A new wiring harness was purchased and installed, and assembly continued with floorboards, some of the wood frame and one seat.

The great day arrived, in December 1999. Jack rigged a temporary battery and ignition wiring, ran the engine, and took his work for a test on his driveway, but that was it for a month, an enforced lay-off when he was diagnosed with a brain tumour. Returning, the engine wouldn't start because the head gasket had leaked. He'd forgotten to re-torque the head after the test drive. A friend told him to use the same copper head gasket but to reanneal it. He did. No leaks.

Now for the bodywork. He replaced all the plywood with birch aircraft plywood, about ten percent of the wood frame but none of the sheet metal. This was cleaned with an electrolytic lye solution, as described in *Skinned Knuckles* magazine, a very slow but gentle process. All that was needed now were patches for the lower rear corners of the quarter panels and the rear end of one fender.

Midway through that he received from Anthony Keator, son of the earlier owner, the original licence plate MG 3945.

All pieces to be painted were trial fitted and adjusted before priming with catalysed filler-primer, sanded, and primed again until smoothness was satisfactory. Colours were to be Oxford and Cambridge blues as described in Malcolm Green's book *MG Road Cars Volume I*. Jack had not spray painted, other than with a can, for about forty years and never with a HVLP spray gun. So he learned as he went along,

The faith of would-be MG owners never fails to lift the spirits. Here and on opposite page, in June 1994, Jack Hardy and wife Sherri are at the beginning of their journey with their 1935 PA. Bought in Nevada City, California and taken to their home in Monrovia CA, PA1875 looks to have kept her personality intact after a very hard life.

Australia, USA and on the high seas, those MGs are everywhere.

Angeles National Forest
7000 ft.

Jack Hardy's PA being met by Canadian border police.

Jack Hardy with his beloved PA, restoration complete.

reading and practising, having trouble with the orange-peel effect, and sagging in places, but getting over his problems.

On 10 June 2001 with everything else installed and all wiring completed and tested, it was time for the open road. Up and down the street it all seemed fine, so Sherri got in, they went a couple of blocks and the oil pump seized. It was not too far to push, but it was uphill.

The cause proved to be bronze gear dust in the oil. A touch of minor panic set in and many different answers were tried. Eventually, after an expert drilled a couple of extra holes in the pump to allow more oil to the driven gears' shaft, it was decided that Jack was being too cautious and the particles were nothing more than normal break-in wear. It took a microscope to see them anyway. He continued driving and checking and changing the oil and filter at 500 miles, and the particles disappeared.

The eight-year job was done, with help and advice from scores of amateur and professional MG folk, and the result was splendid indeed, so splendid that the car was given a part (non-speaking) in the George Clooney film *The Good German*.

Jack Hardy's brain tumour came back and he died in November 2006 at the age of sixty-six. He always wanted the car to be driven, not trailered, and the family take her to events throughout the western USA and Canada, still winning prizes as she did in Jack's day.

Wife Sherri loves the car just as much.

CHAPTER TWENTY THREE

Any Colour, as Long as it's Black or White

A seventeen year old Australian called Thomas Aczel had worked as a builder's labourer over several summer vacations and saved enough money, he thought, to buy a car. He liked the idea of an Austin Healey or a Triumph TR4 but current examples of these types in his price range seemed to have too much wrong with them. Inspected by Tom's father, a professional motor mechanic, each potential purchase was dismissed as too risky. The idea, after all, was for university-bound son to be self-sufficient with the car, not pleading with his dad all the time to fix it.

This was January 1970. At a car auction, outside in the yard, they happened to come across a fairly tired looking 1965 MGB, a white one, which had failed to attract a buyer at the last auction. Father liked the look of it, and a later close inspection in the workshop confirmed his view. It was mechanically sound, and a short test drive with Tom as passenger convinced them both. 'Buy this car,' said father. 'Yes, dad,' said Tom and, after handing over all his savings, A$1,675, it was his.

It is a common failing among grumpy old men these days to say rude things about boy racers. We never drove like maniacs with disco music blasting loud enough to be heard in the next parish, we say, quite forgetting that the only reason we didn't

do that was because we couldn't afford a car. Or, if we could, it was a second-hand Morris Minor, top speed 60mph with a following wind, and it didn't have a radio, much less a million watt stereo sound system.

But, in 1970, with careful financial husbandry, it was possible, as we have seen, for the younger generation to buy a reasonably unlovely specimen of a powerful sports car. Just how powerful, this lad Tom had not yet discovered, but that situation was about to change.

A few weeks into the novel experience of automobile ownership, he was doodling along in the summer sun (Australia, remember), over the bridge from Bondi, up the highway, no particular place to go. The Newcastle Expressway seemed like a good idea but it turned out to be rather boring, a more or less empty, wide, straight road, so Tom put his foot down a bit, and a bit more.

With his foot flat on the floor the rev counter was shivering on the edge of red and the speedo was showing 104mph. As the P (for Provisional) plate on the front of his car indicated, Tom was a driver of less than one year's experience and so was limited to 50mph. He should also have had a P-plate on the back but he hadn't worked out yet how to fix it on without scratching the paint.

Despite the excitement of doing over the ton, Tom happened to notice a large kind of a fellow in a yellow Mini going the other way, giving him a look. Tom thought no more about it as, a few minutes later, he slowed down and came up to traffic. In his mirror, he saw the same yellow Mini, actually a Cooper S, the driver of which was wearing a uniform.

On the day specified in his summons to appear before the beak at Gosford District Court, Tom put on suit and tie and headed thereto, obeying all speed limits and with P-plates affixed. Almost there, and for no reason that he could see, he was pulled over by the police.

'Anything wrong, sir?' asked the lad.

'Don't know yet, do we?' said the officer as he wandered slowly around the vehicle. This was clearly a policeman who expected the worst when boy and fast car were in combination. 'Aha,' he said, cheerfully. 'Have you checked your rear offside tyre lately? I've seen more tread on a boiled egg. I do hope your spare isn't in the same condition.'

Tom had no idea what condition his spare was in but, thankfully, it was revealed as almost new.

'Going far, are we?'

'Only to Gosford, sir.'

'Change your tyre when you get there. And make sure you do, or you'll be going to Gosford again, only this time to the District Court.'

The magistrate in charge of the speeding case (a grumpy old man) listened to the boy's protestations that he had been clocked officially at only 65 mph in a 60 limit, which was admittedly faster than permitted but not by much, and less than everyone else was allowed, and, yes, he had failed to display his rear P-plate but they were very difficult to secure on an MGB. Besides, in a few weeks' time, his provisional year would be up and he'd be allowed to go at 60 on that road. As Master Shakespeare put it in *King Lear*, 'The gods are just, and of our pleasant vices make instruments to plague us'. As the magistrate put it, six months ban and a breathtaking fine.

One of the instruments that can plague MGB owners is the exhaust, so easy to rip off on rough roads. Tom did it twice on country tracks and once on a level

Fully restored to youth and beauty, Tom Aczell's MGB is more than ready for her third trip around the clock, and the next generation of Aczells are already infected with the MG bug.

MGA S-16378 was built in Zetland, Sydney NSW in June 1962 and rebuilt by Brian Barford from the chassis up, and painted black, in Queensland. Now she lives with Tom Aczel in Kurrajong Heights, back in New South Wales and not all that far from where she began. Kurrajong Heights, incidentally, is a village of about 900 people, noted for its annual Back to Back competition. Entrants have to shear a sheep and knit a jumper from the wool in less than a day.

crossing, so thoroughly that the car was stuck. Edging forward or back, the tail pipe or engine pipe would dig in to the railway's stony ground. The thought of their impending doom, crushed to atoms by the next express train, rendered Tom's girlfriend so hysterical that she couldn't even think of saving herself by the simple expedient of getting out of the car and walking five yards.

Tom did get out, to search the boot for ideas and mechanical aid. He found his means of rescue there, a chest expander, which he rigged underneath the car to hold up the tail pipe and so they crept off the railway. Why he should have a chest expander in the boot is a matter that cannot be explained at this distance.

For the next fifteen years, the B was Tom's daily driver, in heatwave or thunderstorm, always reliable, never a let-down, just a bit of rust in the body panels, that's all, until father decided it needed an engine rebuild and rebore at 91,000 miles.

However, much later, at 220,000, the old girl was looking as if she might be past it. Three expensive but rather poorly executed restorations over the years had left Tom with a car he could never part with, because it was part of him, yet one that looked so sad, with wonky panels and peeling paint, that he had to avert his eyes when climbing in. Another restoration might have seemed like throwing good money after bad but he was lucky with the restorer this time. What began to emerge was an extraordinary transformation from rust, filler, chicken wire and other numerous bodges and short cuts to a car that an ex-BMC production engineer marvelled at, saying they could never get the body gaps that good at the factory.

As the restoration progressed, Tom became steadily more involved, and would take small items away to restore himself as a weekend pastime in his neighbour's well equipped workshop, which was great until the job was finished and there was nothing left to do. So, what next? Dear reader, you know the answer. Another MG.

His first thoughts were of a later model MGB to convert to a V8. This idea dimmed in brilliance when it was pointed out that the finished article would look like the first car, only with added possibilities of losing one's driving licence (again). T series MGs were undeniably lovely, but slow in today's traffic. So, what about an MGA? Surely this was the prettiest car ever, and mechanically similar to the MGB he was familiar with.

Almost immediately, he came across an MGA twin cam that had been modified by fitting a Toyota twin cam engine and matching five-speed gearbox. As was known at the time, the original MG twin cam engine had had significant problems. This Toyota thing sounded pretty good, though. There was twin cam yet trouble-free performance and, if anyone criticised him, he could say 'Not guilty, your honour. It weren't me what did it'.

The vendor was not forthcoming about the car's history, but Tom's researches on the internet led him to the car's previous owner. A phone call confirmed that while it was indeed sound, straight and should be rust free, the structural modifications to fit the new engine and gearbox would mean it couldn't be registered in Tom's home state of New South Wales.

Disappointment turned to butterflies when the chap on the phone, Brian Barford, said he just happened to have an MGA for sale, a 1962 1600 Mark I, 50,000 miles from new. It was in Queensland. Tom flew up the next weekend.

Brian Barford had owned seventeen MGAs in his lifetime, plus other MGs, and an early E-type Jag that he'd had for thirty seven years. Very sadly, he was afflicted with a degenerative condition in his eyes and could soon expect to be almost blind. He'd been forced to hand in his driving licence and dispose of his beloved sports cars. As he got in the A beside Tom, he said this would probably be his last ever drive in an MG.

Tom bought it on the spot. Included without being previously mentioned came a treasure trove of spare engine, gearbox, differential, doors, seats, grille, dashboard, crates of smaller parts, MG magazines and the workshop manual.

Tom has found the A to be an interesting surprise. The driving experience he says is remarkably different to the B, given the similar mechanicals and under-pinnings, with a much more vintage feel from the cramped cockpit and steering wheel close to the chest. Those outrageously curved mudguards continue to excite whenever he looks behind to change lanes and, unlike the B, the A is often surrounded by admirers when it's parked. All manner of passing car drivers give a wave or a thumbs-up as they go by.

In other ways too, the MGA has fulfilled Tom's hopes. While completely rust free and straight, she's not perfect so, rather than a concourse car to wash and polish, he has another long-term project with lots of minor details to keep him busy for years to come.

Aubergines a mite less unctuous, please

In a more equitable world, rates of income tax would be set, not according to the amount of income but by the relative usefulness or uselessness of the way it is earned. Lower rates of tax would apply to bin men, brewers, nurses, authors, mechanics and the woman who has the sandwich shop across the road, while much higher rates would act as a continuous reality check on marketing executives, literary agents, cooking sauce endorsers, bankers and motoring journalists.

The latter may plead partial exemption due to the impossibility of their task, that is, to find something interesting and different to say about this week's new car, which is indistinguishable from last week's. As restaurant critics, embroiled in an endless sequence of free banquets, are reduced to remarking on a slight grittiness in the lentil-stuffed pig's trotters, or a suspicion of over-unctuousness in the *Khatte Baigan**, so car reviewers become increasingly desperate for anything halfway sensible to say.

'The stalk for wipers and indicators did its business with a Teutonic snap,' wrote one of a car costing £50,000. 'The steering was exact and firmly communicative.' Well, there's a funny thing.

Perhaps that reviewer should have driven your correspondent's first vehicle, a fifth-hand 1966 Bedford minibus. 'Having driven from London, stopping off at the transport caff at Cannock Chase, we approached Rhydlanfair on the A5. The brakes failed entirely. With another ten twisting, mountainous miles to go to Capel Curig, in the dark, I wondered idly if this inconvenience would make us too late for the pub. After a severe testing of the gears, and of steering which compared unfavourably in speed of response with that of the Runcorn ferry, I overshot the campsite gate by a few feet. My companions awoke from their sleep to point this out.'

By working their Saturday afternoon off, the two garage men of Capel Curig qualified with knobs on for the Equitable Income Tax, replacing all manner of perished hydraulic pipes and charging nine quid.

(*For those who do not read the restaurant columns, this is Kashmiri sour aubergines.)

CHAPTER TWENTY FOUR

Baby, Come Back

Colin Baldry's first MG was a 1966 B Roadster, bought second-hand in 1978 when he was 21, ECF 671D, or Eastern Counties Farmers as he thought of it, being from Suffolk. He wanted a sports car, simple as that, and the B was reasonably priced, or cheap, even, so he got it even though he had to wait a year, to his 22nd birthday, before he could afford the insurance to drive it.

It had the blue leather upholstery and the blue hood but the body had been resprayed in Ford silver fox. An American airman based at RAF Bentwaters in

Colin may not want to renovate a car himself but houses, well, that's a different story. This is his sixteenth-century Suffolk cottage, much improved in the view of a previous owner by the uPVC windows, Fletton brick chimney stack, rendering over the timber frame, plastic conservatory and roof remade to a shallower pitch (the house would have been thatched originally). The car is 1966. The house is circa 1566. The car is as was. So will be the house.

Suffolk bought that car from him, so it might be in the States now, and Colin replaced it with a 1972 Mark III Midget, square rear wheel arches, hood attached to car.

The hood was detached from the car when a speedster came hurtling down Fore Street in Framlingham, just as Colin was emerging cautiously from a junction. Caution is no use when encountering maniacs and so the Midget was crushed against a wall and Colin was lucky to get out.

Two years later he took on another B Roadster, 1975 model, with rubber bumpers and overdrive control on the wiper switch, which he swapped after another two years for a 1973 Midget, round wheel arches, and £1,000. The money was needed to go towards buying his first flat, in Richmond, and the car made up for its lack of performance versus the B by its terrific noise. It had a Janspeed log centre branch manifold, mated to a straight-through exhaust. Colin's flatmate swore he could hear every gear change as far away as Chiswick.

That car had to go and, apart from one year with a Midget Mark IV, the 1500, rubber bumpers (actually plastic) and square rear wheel arches, which he gave as a present to his girlfriend, that was it for a while. He became unfaithful, and hitched up with modern sports cars by TVR, Mazda and Porsche until, overcome by nostalgia, he fell for a nearly-MG, a 1971 Austin Healey Sprite.

Colin has no pretensions to advanced mechanicism and no wish to build a car out of a box of bits found in a barn, so when he replaced the Sprite it had to be with a B somebody else had restored, and it had to be a D reg, just like his first one.

Come on, boss. Never mind having our picture taken. Let's be going.

CHAPTER TWENTY FIVE

You Can Take the Boy Out of the MG

…but you can't take the MG-ness out of the boy, as this story demonstrates.

The first car in which Bob McCluskey had any nominal equity was an Austin 7 saloon, a 1932 Ruby, which he was supposed to own jointly with his brother. Brother counted it as his, took it with him to university and Bob never saw it again. Next was a 1937 Morris 8 two-seater tourer, registration DXX 778. Although not a consideration in the purchase at the time, such a car was also owned by the son of Emperor Haile Selassie and was Colin Chapman's first car in 1945. Bob's parents sourced his in 1960 from a sergeant in the RAF who was being posted away and took £10 for it. It turned out to be excellent value for money.

Bob learned that into this two-seater you could fit six university students, or two students and two firkins of beer. It had an upper speed limit of about 60mph, which meant he could become illegal by the top of The Avenue in Southampton if he could get a running start without having to stop at the traffic lights at the bottom.

Bob also learned a lot about mechanics and how to coax reluctant engines into life. He learned how to line-ream kingpin bushes, and what makes axles whine, and how to coddle white-metal big ends, and he learned that after the journals have been ground so many times that the crankshaft looks like a coat hanger, the metal can squeeze out of the bearings like toothpaste.

The second time this happened, he was far from home with no money. He took off the sump, drew out the con-rod and piston, covered the oilway in the journal with a jubilee clip and a bit of leather cut off his belt, and drove home on three cylinders. From this he adduced that oil in your hair and eyes is no fun, and that the police really don't like the smoke that comes from having the oil mist in the sump connected directly to the exhaust valves.

In a Morris 8 one can do very satisfying four-wheel drifts around corners when there is no friction with the road surface because the tyres are worn down to canvas. There are other similarities to MGs as well, including identical Silentravel door latches. When Bob's passenger door latch disappeared, one of the previously unreliable MGs around the campus suddenly had doors that shut. He should have stolen it back but instead settled for a bolt, but this could rattle open, so it was supplemented with string across to the steering column.

When carrying a passenger this couldn't work, so her job was to hold the door closed. One day, driving through the narrow Somerset lanes with their high hedges, Bob came a little close to one of the hedges and his passenger let go of the door. The door swung open and scooped half a hundredweight of Somerset hedgerow into the back of the car, cracking the rear door pillar timber, and the door never closed properly again. Thereafter it was kept shut with a padlock and hasp, and passengers had to climb over the door or scramble in over the driver's seat.

Another endearing feature that no twenty-first century boy racer could possibly appreciate, was in the headlight system. Rules then only required that cars had a single nearside headlight, set so it didn't dazzle oncoming traffic. On main beam, both headlights would be on, illuminating the road as well as two glow-worms could, but when you dipped the lights the offside one would go out and, with a loud spark and a slight electrical smell of ozone, a solenoid would move the whole nearside light – bulb, reflector, and all – so that it pointed at the ground just in front of the wheels, leaving the driver effectively in the dark.

This car lasted Bob all the way through undergraduate studies and well into his first job, as a circuit design engineer on the TSR2, the world's first supersonic swing-wing fighter plane. He felt his status demanded a more professional image and imagined this could be achieved by driving an MG. He borrowed £100 from the bank and bought a TC. The day before he was to take delivery, the owner ran it into the garage door and dented the front mudguard. Bob negotiated the price down to £70 on that account, and drove it back to the cottage he was sharing in Bushey Heath.

There, he realised from the sliding trunnions that it wasn't a TC at all, but the rarest T type, the much more desirable TB. This was quite a coincidence, because one of three housemates also had a TB, so between them they had two of the 379 TBs ever made, or 0.53 percent. Bob remembers feeling pretty smug. He had a wondrous car plus an unexpected £30 worth of beer vouchers. He gave the Morris away to somebody in the pub while redeeming some of vouchers.

As well as the XPAG engine, which made its first appearance in the TB and stayed all the way through to the MGA, still leaking oil onto the clutch through the rear oil seal, the TB had some truly marvellous attributes. For example, under the bonnet was an array of nipples, with copper tubes running back to all the lubrication points on the suspension, legacy of MGs way back to the J2: you could service the whole car from one spot. You could see in the dark with Lucas King of the Road eight-inch dual filament lights, and there was no petrol gauge, and no petrol warning light, like the TCs. What it did have was a fuel reserve. When you ran out you turned a tap on the dashboard for another four gallons.

Alas, it was but nine months until the TB met her destiny on the old A1 at Barnet. In the first few light drops of rain after the long, hot, dry summer of 1964, the oily road became slippery. TB and driver drifted gently but inexorably into oncoming traffic. Nowadays the damage would seem trivial to Bob, to be fixed in a couple of weekends. Then it seemed irredeemable. He sold the wreck for an unremembered sum but which proved sufficient for the fine and £25 left over.

Since the 1932 J2 only cost £20, the sun had got his hat on again. Bob perfected the no-clutch gear change, against the day when the clutch might not work, and enjoyed the speedo which was really a tacho, showing estimated speeds according to revs and which gear he was in. Mechanically there were many drawbacks, or eccentricities, but all could be lived with, once understood, but the angel of death hovered near.

Bob drove to Staines to an MG wrecker for a part, making a long trip for this little battler. As he came into the yard, the engine made a loud mechanical noise and stopped abruptly. The man convinced Bob that the overhead valves were notoriously unreliable, and one of them had dropped onto the piston beneath. He revealed a row of ten J2s and said they all had dropped valves. Bob's car was

Once upon a time in Australia, there was an MG TD.

Bob McCluskey's 1952 TD, as a work in progress and as a work of art.

therefore worthless. Out of the kindness of his heart, the man gave Bob £5 for the remains, so he hitch-hiked back into London and spent the five quid on beer.

There followed a series of mistakes, beginning with a Berkeley, a tiny, frog-eyed, vaguely E-typeish ahead of its time car, powered by a motorcycle engine and built by Berkeley Caravans to a Lawrie Bond design. Bob's vehicle seized after ten miles.

Then there was the Markham-Peasey Sabre, another piece of 1950s futuristics, which had no doors and an all-in-one moulded body shell, so it was like driving around in Dan Dare's bathtub. Bob was caught in a thunderstorm near Winchester, in a typical bank holiday traffic jam, with no-one moving. The car began to fill up with water. He punched holes in the floor with a screwdriver to let it out and said goodbye soon afterwards.

The last mistake was a Ginetta G2, a kit car which looked rather like a Lotus (as in Lots Of Trouble, Usually Serious) Six crossed with a dog. There were several unfortunate incidents, culminating in a hot sunny dawn somewhere in the New Forest. 'Hot' and 'dawn' is not a usual collocation and Bob was musing on this unusual meteorological feature when he realised that the heat was coming, not from the sun, but from a gallon of Duckham's 20W/50 pumped all over his trousers.

Bob McCluskey came to Sydney in 1969 as a ten-pound Pom. Compared to home, the public transport seemed inadequate and the climate benevolent, so an open-top sports tourer was indicated. Inquiries produced no TCs so he settled on a TD, bought in his first week, for a month's salary.

Bob felt in the same way about this car as modern drivers might feel about their Toyotas and whatnot: car works for owner, not owner for car. In view of his car-owning history, we may wonder at his optimism: car, works? The TD, Bob thought, was already middle-aged and unattractive; she was too old to be sexy, too knocked about to be glamorous. He gave her just enough attention to keep her running, but not enough to keep her running well, and gradually she decayed into her seventh age, 'sans teeth, sans eyes, sans taste, sans everything'.

The fabric of the hood shrank until it missed the windscreen by several inches, so for several years afterwards the car was driven open regardless of the weather. At one time she had a cement mixer in the back, another time half a cubic yard of topsoil. The back bumper was removed so Bob could fit a tow bar for his dinghy, and all the while she lived on the street, around the corner from the pub, and therefore suffered scratches and dings as patrons negotiated their way home at closing time, or bus drivers got careless. Bits were replaced as they were damaged or corroded beyond repair, even some of the timber when the doors stopped shutting, but none of it was done with care and high regard.

After seven years, Bob re-emigrated – Oz to UK – thinking never to return. He left the car with a friend to sell, and heard no more of it in the nine years it took him to decide to re-re-emigrate, with wife Margaret and a Lotus Seven. His friend heard he was back and made contact. He'd thought Bob was going for a holiday and he was to look after the car for a few weeks, but it was still there, in the back paddock.

Oh dear. The car had had a cover but that had blown off several years before. Leaves had piled up in every possible nook and cranny: behind and around the windscreen pillars and scuttle, between the front valence and radiator grille, around the headlight brackets, between the sweep of the front mudguards and the bonnet, behind the spare wheel carrier...everywhere imaginable, including in the doors, the trim having been removed in the bodged attempt to replace the timbers and, characteristically, never replaced.

These leaves had performed their very own prehistoric chemical reaction. High-class leaf-mould had combined with the salt in the air of the NSW north coast to form an oxidising agent, too powerful for objects made by feeble Man. The only items to survive the onslaught were the bonnet, which had a covering of oil and grease inside and no niches for leaves outside, and most of the chassis, which was likewise covered in oil and grease thanks to the XPAG rear oil seal.

Rats had nested in the upholstery and gnawed through the wiring harness. The floorboards had largely disappeared into dust. A young wattle (acacia tree, floral symbol of Australia known for rapid growth but short life) was thrusting through the chassis members. Numerous wood-boring insects had raised their young in the frame timbers.

The wattle was sawn off and a forklift put the car onto a trailer for the journey back to Sydney. There she stayed in the garden under a tarpaulin, degenerating further for a couple of years. Finally, Bob decided he should do something to save this gentlewoman in distress. He got a quote from a professional which quickly clarified the first issue: if the car were to be restored, Bob would have to learn how to do it himself.

But what sort of restoration? A car for everyday use, leaving commuters and Sunday drivers gasping in disbelief and envy? Or a concourse job? How much to spend? Where to draw the line between original components and replacements?

Bob was not a fan of concourse cars. They seemed to him to spend too much time under covers, coming out occasionally for club meets, maybe even brought and taken home on a trailer, with no proof they actually ran. They used modern paints, modern oil seals, hydraulics, pistons, gaskets, and bearings, yet they were often judged largely on originality, like the engine colour must be matched, and the number of fasteners on the tonneau must be correct. He'd heard the judges at a concourse discussing whether there was enough yellow in the colour of the rocker box cover, which to him seemed an anorak too far.

He would be guided by what he thought Cecil Kimber would have wanted; a car to drive. He would use existing components where possible. He would be reasonably faithful to the original design, but would take advantage of the best of modern materials or components where this was a consideration, noting that modern systems are usually more reliable and often cheaper than second-hand originals or replicas. He would feel free to modify components to improve reliability, comfort, and appearance, in that order. He would not be constrained by the paint colours of austere postwar Britain, but probably wouldn't use metallics nor have paint flames coming from the bonnet louvres.

He would ensure that the car was dignified and unmistakably an MG, and not a modern replica and, as far as was reasonable, if reason came into it, he would do it himself. This would be his car and he would enjoy it, irrespective of complete approval from purists.

The story of the restoration is a very detailed one and a template for any who would consider embarking on such a project. To examine this textbook case, go to http://members.optusnet.com.au/bobmccluskey.

CHAPTER TWENTY SIX

Who Is Rarest Of Them All?

Pete Thelander was stationed in Augsburg, Germany with the US Army when he bought his first MG in 1956. It was a 1954 TF with 16,000 miles on the clock. He drove it over the Alps to Innsbruck, on to Venice, Rome and Naples, up the Italian Riviera to Monaco and returned over the Alps to Bavaria. Later trips took him to Amsterdam and Paris. The Army would ship a car home for all returning GIs, so it came back with him when his tour of duty was over and here he had his first major failure. On the way from New York to Chicago, it ran a rod bearing near Cleveland and spent the final 300 miles on a rope behind an Austin Healey.

He repaired the rod bearing and sold the car to raise funds for the start of married life with Fran, but wedded bliss ex-MG lasted only a year. They saw the very same car at a dealer's in Chicago, bought it back and have never been without an MG since.

He drove Fran to the hospital in the TF for the birth of their first child, and brought them both home in it, but the imminence of number two forced Pete to think about a nice family saloon. It would not be a typical soft-sprung American

Pete Thelander's TF, his first MG of many, in German snow, 1956.

After curing the dodgy steering, the TC became Pete and Fran Thelander's favourite travelling machine. Here it is in the 21st century, at 8000 feet on the Tioga Pass in Yosemite National Park.

Pete and Fran overtake a local bicycle at the Ards Tourist Trophy 75th anniversary, 2003.

All seven of the E variant of the N-type Magnette are still extant, although two are yet to be restored. Pete Thelander is compiling the definitive NE dossier, as restorer/owner of 20 per cent of the world's going population.

boat, however, but one of a new race of US automobiles, the sporty compact, the Chevrolet Corvair Monza, all be it with family concessions as in station-waggon model. After two winters in New England, he took a job in California and towed the TF to LA by Corvair power.

Over the next several years, Pete found himself acquiring stray MGs, mostly TDs, to fix up and sell, in a sort of reality TV pilot for the British programme *Wheeler Dealer*. At one point he had thirteen MGs around the place; then came one of those moments. In 1972, while tracking down a TA Tickford that was allegedly going for nothing, he was put on the trail of a 1934 MG NE Magnette. Not really knowing what it was, he went to look. This magnificent beast, the racing model of the N-type of which only seven were built, could be his at about the going rate for a working-order TC and, well, it was just too tempting. He drove it home but it never was reliable, always temperamental, running for a short while and then inexplicably dying.

The problem in fact was rust in the tank that would pile up and block the fuel line, but at that time Pete wasn't confident enough to tackle NE surgery. He felt rather intimidated by the mechanical peculiarities of this thoroughbred, so very different from the T-series MGs he had been dealing with. Eventually the engine seized and it sat neglected for quite number of years while the family grew up.

With some MG friends, Pete and Fran founded the Vintage MG Club of Southern California, which is still going strong after almost forty years with 200 members. Likewise with help from fellow MG fans, and encouragement from Al Moss (founder of Moss Motors), they organised the first Gathering of the Faithful for all the vintage MG clubs in the western United States. This event has been held every year since and has taken everyone on some of the most enjoyable trips possible, and to places they probably would never have seen otherwise.

In 1974, Pete landed a TC with the engine in pieces on the front seat. He figured it would be easier to sell if it was running but, once he did get it going, he experienced the dodgy steering that was part of the TC's reputation. Little by little, he found things in the steering and front end that needed attention and, with such matters resolved, found it very enjoyable to drive. He never did sell it. Rather, it was driven to most of the GoF Wests. The Thelanders have done 100,000 miles in it.

Restoring the NE was always on the to-do list, but family came first and, as the three offspring – Pete junior, Joe and Peggy – became car drivers, a family car pool was a necessity. It couldn't be the usual thing with semi-expendable Euro-boxes and other anonymous vehicles, so it consisted of a 1962 MGA Mark II fixed head coupé, a 1967 MGB GT and a 1969 MGC GT. All three cars accumulated over 100,000 miles.

With the nest empty, it was finally time to get serious about restoring the NE and about using it as intended. The job took a year, interrupted by a mild heart attack, but Pete was much more confident now. His optimism was a little shaken when the man to whom he'd subcontracted the engine-build announced that he had to disappear suddenly. There were two engines as raw material; Pete took them home and began sorting what amounted to two jigsaw puzzles in the same box. He began without knowing which bit went with what.

He took his completed car to a couple of training exercises with VARA at Willow Springs and Phoenix International Raceway and was then accepted for the Monterey Historic Automobile Races. He's taken part in three or four events a year ever since.

The Ulster Vintage Car Club decided to hold a 75th Anniversary Commemoration of the Ards Tourist Trophy races outside Belfast, Northern Ireland, in 2003. This was the race for which the NE was created, after they barred the supercharged K. Pete had heard of the 50th and 65th anniversary events and had vowed to make the next. It took a lot of planning and co-ordination, but they were there with the car. It certainly was one of the highlights of their MG life.

As if all that were not enough, Pete bought a 1934 PA roadster which supposedly had not run in thirty or forty years. It's running now, and is drivable, unlike the faithful retainer TF, inoperable after an engine fire, and the C has sadly fallen into disuse due to mechanical problems he hasn't found time to sort out.

The TC, the driving favourite, goes on and on, taking Pete and Fran from Los Angeles up to Canada and the northwest US five or six times. Al Moss and Pete drove it across the US some three thousand miles each way to an eastern GoF in Killington, Vermont in New England in just two weeks.

Beat that, T Bird.

CHAPTER TWENTY SEVEN

Love Story

Gerry Graham grew up in Dubbo, New South Wales, during the 1940s and 50s, a time when they had a shed instead of a garage and a wash house instead of a laundry, and when dinner was eaten in the middle of the day (only posh people ate lunch and had dinner at tea-time). Regardless of social niceties, the wool industry was booming and the boomers had lots of money to spend on interesting cars. Gerry remembers an XK120 that would park in his street, an Allard throwing dirt and grass up at a gymkhana, a couple of Mark I Jaguars, a Triumph Mayflower, a 2.5 Riley, lots of Healeys, TRs and, of course, MGs.

'My first real love was the TF. Although I was only a kid, I would con a ride in a TF or any MG as often as possible, and even learned the art of the double shuffle, as drivers proudly found first gear without making crunching noises. I was so entranced that I stopped drawing Spitfires in my schoolbooks and started drawing TFs.'

Gerry backed his starry eyedness with practical measures, taking a holiday job at age fourteen in a car repair shop. One day a TF was brought in with a dropped valve. The owner had been belting it around a dirt track oval and had held it at high revs too long. Gerry was deeply resentful. How could anyone able to live his dream of owning a T, betray the dream in such a way? How could anyone inflict so much pain on this beautiful lady? And then came his Damascene moment.

'Late in 1955, I came out of church one Sunday morning to find, parked across the road, a new type of sports car. I rushed across to look. It had the MG octagon, it was an MG, but where were the running boards, the slab tank, the external spare wheel, the long straight bonnet, the vertical grille, the fold-flat windscreen, the cutaway suicide doors? And it was pale blue. No TF was ever that colour.

'This apparition was an MGA. I felt cheated and abandoned. Why would they change everything when there were plenty of letters left to follow the F, such as G, H, I and J? I tried to draw the new car in my sketchbook but I couldn't.'

In 1960, Gerry went to Sydney Teachers' College on a scholarship. It was a big step for a country boy, but he soon felt at home as one student had a TF and another had a TC. There wasn't enough in the Graham wallet to join them so he bought a 1937 Morris 8/40 for £27, almost one month's scholarship money. It had a straight-through exhaust, a burned exhaust valve, extremely vague steering and brakes, and a battery that only stayed charged if he wound the third brush on the generator all the way forward. The roof leaked and the windscreen went opaque in the rain, but Gerry was eighteen, and it did look a bit like an MG.

He sold it for a tenner when he went on his first teaching job, in Cobar, New South Wales, and saved up for a deposit on his dream car. He considered a frog-eyed Sprite (too small), a big Healey (too expensive, and the rear was too low for the bush) or a Morgan (a bone shaker), giving no thought to a Morris Minor or a VW Beetle. After deep cogitation, a conclusion was reached. It had to be a TF1500.

'Off to Sydney I went in September 1962. I knew almost nothing about cars and had no one to guide me. There was no shortage of TF1250s for around £350 but the only example of the rarer 1500 was at a BMC dealer's in Neutral Bay. There she was, in the showroom on a display ramp, under spotlights. The Lady in Red. I was transfixed, besotted, also very young and very green, and agreed to a whopping price of £575.

'Never mind. I was now a member of the Worshipful Company of MG Brethren. I could use the secret sign (a slight elevation of the index finger from the steering wheel as another MG approached) and I could proudly drive my lady home to Dubbo. My mother said it looked like my last car, 'the Morris 8.'

Over the next months at his new teaching job in the Australian outback, Gerry learned many interesting things about his car and went on a self-inflicted crammer course in car mechanics. The cluster gear and clutch were both fit for the knacker and, would you believe it, his genuine TF1500 body was fitted with a 1250 engine. He had paid more than two hundred pounds over the odds. After hearing Gerry's moans and groans and fierce denunciations, the BMC dealer brought his attention to an old Latin saying enshrined at that time in the law – *Caveat Emptor*, 'let the buyer beware' – and switched into Anglo-Saxon when the lad complained again.

Gerry got to work on a sandy bit of waste ground outside the boarding house where he was living.

'The first thing was lack of oil pressure, so off came the sump, and the bearings looked like the surface of the moon. I replaced them, but not before the sand got in and the small child from next door came to help me by shuffling the bearing caps (I didn't know about witness marking then). Next came the clutch replacement, which on a TF is much easier than a B because the engine does not have to come out, and I noticed that my rear tyres were wearing on the inside. TFs don't have independent rear suspension do they? No, but they do have axle tubes that are shrink fitted to the diff housing, which work loose. I jacked up the car by the diff, and both axle tubes could be moved up and down. So I phoned Sportscar Spares, who sent me out by train a second-hand housing, the inside of which looked like a hand grenade had exploded in it. But it was fine, so I fitted my old crown wheel and pinion and all was well.'

Well, Gerry, they do say the course of true love never runs smooth. After a small electrical fire behind the dashboard, Gerry was driving along when he noticed the oil gauge flicker and go to zero. He'd changed the oil and filter that day and hadn't sealed the cartridge cover properly. It was a long walk home. But help was at hand. The father of one of the kids he taught was a top pro mechanic.

'He wouldn't do things for me; he made me do it, and would watch and correct my mistakes. I disassembled the TF motor, including the camshaft and bearings, and successfully put it all back together again, and fitted a new second-hand crankshaft. So confident was I that I almost took on a PB that I saw on a sheep station, slowly recycling itself into the environment under a pepper tree. No one really knew what it was and no one valued or claimed it. It was just abandoned like the rest of the broken farm machinery. I could have had it for nothing, but where would I put it? I was only twenty one and continually flat broke because of the demands of my TF, and I could only afford one mistress. So I replaced the TF's windscreen that had been peppered by many stones, resprayed her to British Racing Green, had a sexy new tonneau cover made, paid off the last instalment and, in 1965, traded my lady CLK 014 for a Mini. Now followed my wilderness years, featuring a Renault Dauphine.

'And then, one enchanted evening in 1968 in a narrow back lane in Paddington, I saw her, unwanted and unloved, a real TF1500. Both front guards and the grille were badly damaged, the dumb irons a bit bent, rubbish had accumulated around the wheels, she had Victorian number plates, and seemed to have been abandoned.

'I enquired at the local police station. The car had been reported as a nuisance by neighbours. I could take it away if I left my name and address in case the owner turned up. Well, he turned up a few days later wanting $200. Cheap at the price.'

The bodywork timber was in good condition except for the doors, and other bits and pieces were found reasonably easily. The engine had seized, but after many days of penetrating oil, gentle pressure and tapping, it came free and was not in too bad condition and, after many, many hours of work there came the reward.

'My first proper drive revealed just how much more powerful she was than the 1250. It all came flooding back. Windscreen wiper switches in glove box, fly-off hand brake, large convex driver's mirror, doors that threatened to fly open without warning, side-screens that bellied out at speed, fold-down windscreen, rev counter that worked off the generator and was only as accurate as the tightness of the fan belt, a very hot left foot, the funny little accelerator roller pedal but, most of all, the long bonnet with a front view of that lovely chrome octagon, and sexy mudguards. I was deeply in love again.'

The only drawback was the paintwork. It had been red but Gerry was still keen on British Racing Green. He bought some paint that said 'racing green' on the tin, sprayed it, and his friends saluted him as he went past in something the colour of an army staff car.

'It was a tough decision but eventually I had to realise that the need to feed, clothe and provide shelter for my wife Heather and young child was paramount, so I sold AAI 074 to raise the deposit on a house. Alas, the new responsible me didn't last long. Withdrawal symptoms forced me into buying the car I still have today, my real and lasting true love, my old white B, 1967. She wasn't always old of course, but she has always been white.'

The car was used as everyday transport until 1980, when the demands of an increased family and two sensible cars meant that it had to be pensioned off. Gerry wouldn't sell but de-registered it, a very sad day, almost like putting down a favoured pet, and borrowed garage space for a couple of years until the sun came out.

'I think it was 1990 when I started a full restoration. The car was completely stripped, including the front mudguards, electrics and brakes. The engine was rebuilt and balanced, and all that needed doing to the gearbox was a new layshaft, bearings and seals. Not bad for 180,000 miles. There was some minor rust and I replaced the affected metal, but the floor was OK. I resprayed the car myself, and had some chrome work done, and the wire wheels trued. My B had to be re-registered, and off I drove to the RTA. "Sir," the man said firmly, "I have to ask you to wait here. This car is reported stolen and I have called the police."'

'I showed him much documentation dating back to 1972, plus their own microfilm of AQC 339 as it was then known, but my tormentor was unmoved. I told him I wasn't waiting for the police to come to me; I was going to them. I drove to the police station, parked my unregistered stolen MG in the Police Parking Only zone, and confessed my crime to the first copper who would listen. He entered some numbers into his computer, and the result was a stolen box trailer.'

Gerry has modified his car for racing, with a gas flowed and valve timed head, a mild 608 cam, bored out and balanced engine, lightened flywheel, 5 speed gearbox from a Nissan Skyline, servo brakes, uprated front springs and larger anti-sway bar and a bit of negative camber. The wire wheels had to go because he kept breaking spokes, even on new wheels, and have been replaced with alloy wheels and sticky semi-racing rubber. It does have a roll bar, but as an old mate said, they look crook, but they work great when you're upside down.

Gerry has competed at every circuit in NSW, including Amaroo Park and Bathurst, as well as Philip Island in Victoria and Simmons Plains in Tasmania, but he says that the best fun is club events and the comradeship of other club members.

'We have a terrific bunch of people who are great companions and supportive friends, and I am very fortunate to have made their acquaintance. All of us enjoy using our MGs in different ways, such as breakfast runs and mid-week musters, but the common thread is the company of like-minded people.'

On the way to teach in an outback school, somewhere deep in New South Wales, Gerry Graham stopped for a break near a village called Nevertire. He had many more miles to go along the Crystal Highway, so called because of the amount of windscreen and headlamp glass littering it, finishing with 30 miles of dirt road that also finished the diff housing.

CHAPTER TWENTY EIGHT

Flivver, Roger, Fran, and Rosy's Revenge

The bus journey into Birmingham for his weekly driving lesson took a seventeen year old engineering apprentice past a car showroom. One day, in that showroom stood a black TC, for sale at £165. It was there the next week too, and the next. Why had nobody bought it? The answer was obvious to the apprentice, Roger Bragger. Nobody had bought it because it was meant for him. The Fates had issued a decree. And at £165, he could borrow the money and afford to pay it back.

Being a sensible lad, Roger decided to sort out the money before going to see the car, and his first approach was not to the bank manager but to his (non-driving) dad.

'So, obviously, you think you're going to pass your test, do you, son?' said father. Roger nodded. 'In which case,' continued the dad, 'such a matter cannot be difficult. So, I shall learn to drive and I shall buy the car for us both to use, only it won't be a two-seater rustbucket flivver designed for turning girls' heads. It will be a reliable family saloon.'

No, it's not a rat's nest, nor have there been chickens living in it. After 30 years, the chipboard that used to line the car's roof has gone back to nature.

Rosy before the treatment. DXW indicates original registration in London.

Job done. No explanation required.

Flivver in Copenhagen.

Roger's dad never did learn to drive. He didn't need to. He had Roger to drive him wherever he wanted to go, and whenever, because he owned the 1959 Mark II Ford Zodiac, the free use of which Roger had otherwise.

Meanwhile, the 167th TA, registration DGH 23, was being driven around Aylesbury and district by a Mr Robert H Wilson, godson of the original owner Mr O'Dell, who probably lived in London, that being the indication of DGH. Wilson sold it to his nephew, Martin W Bastion, for £200, who sold it to Mike Feeny whose intention was to do a full restoration. Feeny stripped it down all right but didn't put it together again, instead selling it in boxes to Ken Williams.

We're in 1985 at this point. By 1989 the Williams restoration was complete, and he ran it for ten years though he didn't run it much. By 1999, the 'new' car had only done 4,100 miles. Roger bought it and he and his wife Fran drove it to Berlin.

He decided to call it Flivver, in memory of his dad, having looked up the word in the dictionary and found it to be American slang for a cheap and rubbishy car or aeroplane.

Two years went by and, mixing with all these MG types in clubs and rallies, Roger began to get the restoration bug. Telling himself that he was only thinking of Fran, who wanted a TA of her own, he tracked one down that had stood in a garage for thirty one years. Amazingly, the tyres inflated and, as it had been left with the brake off and in neutral, it rolled out of the garage and down the drive.

The list of things wrong with this car will be familiar to anyone who has ever tried to do what Roger was planning. All sorts of items, such as lights, had been replaced with incorrect or home-made ones, there was rot and rust throughout, the rear wheels were wrong, the engine was seized, the block was cracked, and all manner of repairs had been bodged. So that was fine, then, and after eight years the car, called Rosy, was finished enough to sit her MOT test.

So far, so normal. Sighs of relief all round, photographs, great senses of satisfaction, et cetera. Little did Roger know that the imps of mischief, during the restoration, had dropped a small nut and bolt into the gearbox.

Several months passed. Finishing touches were applied. Faults were ironed out. Life with Rosy seemed, well, rosy, until one January day on the M42 there was a crunching and a whirring. The noises were disturbing but didn't stop the car, and so Roger had her over the pit at home and drained the oil. With the lubricant, out came a bolt and a washer, both in good condition, a piece of helical gear tooth, and a thoroughly mangled nut. While bolt, washer and nut had remained together, all had been hunky-dory, but the nut had gradually unscrewed itself, been picked up by the gears, and how the imps of mischief laughed.

And they hadn't finished with Roger yet. In reaching out of his pit to grab the handle of a bench-mounted vice that he generally used as an aid to getting in and out, he grabbed the gearbox of his spare engine instead which, at that moment, happened not to have its usual block of wood supporting it.

The engine tilted, fell on to Roger's steel toolbox, crushed it, and then followed him into the pit where it jammed him against the side. He could just reach the chains of his block and tackle and manage to get the engine off him, which had suffered only a few scratches. Roger had a dislocated shoulder and a shoulder blade broken in two places.

As Noggin says on page 89, 'You from OSHA or what?'.

BUILD YOUR OWN MODEL OF THE

M.G. SPORTS CAR!

Here's the ultimate in craftsmanship — a realistic replica of the famous British M.G. — finest model kit ever produced!

This **Model** masterpiece has more than 50 precision-fitted parts, including steerable front wheel assembly, semi-pneumatic tires and semi-elliptical rear springs — yet it requires only a screwdriver for assembly. Body is durable die-cast construction, chassis is heavy steel. Comes with gray primer coat — can be painted to your preference.

An absorbing, educational "father-and-son" project, the **Model MT** is a rugged, thrill-packed toy when assembled — or a handsome collectors' item for sports car owners and hobbyists.

Price   Made by the makers of world famous

$10⁹⁵
West, $11.75

MT SPORTS CAR KIT

DOEPKE **Model** TOYS

FOR FREE CATALOG, WRITE TO:
The CHAS. WM. DOEPKE MFG. CO., INC., ROSSMOYNE 1, OHIO

CHAPTER TWENTY NINE

Come On, Feel The Noise

Terry Cooper of Chelmsford bought his hardtop B as a rolling, painted shell with accompanying boxes of bits. He didn't know whether everything was there or not, or what state it was in. He knew a little about cars and their mechanics but nothing about MGBs and, as he'd never done anything remotely like this before, he had no idea what bits should have been there in the first place. Regardless of such a start from the very back of the grid, he rebuilt the car in his spare time, within a year.

Well, good show, but nothing so remarkable in that, you may say, but you would be wrong. Terry is blind. He can distinguish light from dark but that's all. He was sighted when younger and worked as an engineering machinist before blindness,

The wheels go round and the rest of it is in cardboard boxes. Well, let's hope so.

One man and his B – what's so special about that?

so he did understand the principles at least. He had mechanical advice and words of encouragement from his friend Paul Hunt (see page 27) and others, and Paul did some wiring that required a sighted person to be sure, but otherwise Terry built the car to roadworthiness and an easy MOT pass entirely on his own, purely by touch, memory, and imagination from others' descriptions.

Terry also has a full-time managerial position with social services, looks after his two young children when his partner is at work, does DIY, gardening, and goodness knows what else. And he did something that the great majority of sighted people could not do in a millennium of Sundays, even though he can't drive the damned thing himself.

CHAPTER THIRTY

Rhapsody in Blue

Erik and Pam Benson, Scottish folk who live in France, have 'MG' engraved on their hearts with octagon border, or would have if it were surgically possible. So many MGs have they had, and so many restorations has Erik done, that he's going to write a book about it, one winter, soon, when he's not fiddling with his cars.

Not that Erik is an obsessive, at least not compared with his old Glaswegian pal Ron, who used to appear at MG gatherings in his PA. The rumour was that he had

How many owners has each J2 had? Only 2,083 were made and yet, in Erik Benson's experience, not only has every MG restorer had a Meccano set in his youth, but thousands of them started motor-car life with a J2. This is Erik in 1957, in Glasgow, where it looks like rain, with the J2 half-owned with another student. Equality of opportunity to drive both halves was a matter never resolved to the entire satisfaction of either owner.

Lying second at the moment, Erik Benson races his TC for the first time at Silverstone, 1972. He says he was never wealthy enough to just go out a buy the sports cars he wanted so, like many, he had to learn how to fix them up. Over forty years of T racing brings close friendships, which is perhaps more important than sheer speed.

a huge stash at his house of dismantled old MGs, but no-one had ever been allowed inside to confirm it. Erik's chance came when Ron, in need of some ready cash, asked him if he'd like to buy advance supplies of parts, in case of future need.

It was a big house, on several floors, with a large cellar and a mews garage. The entire place was a pre-war MG graveyard. There was a room full of radiators. There were boxes of bits everywhere. The garage had two piles of axles, back and front, going right up to ceiling. Erik saw twenty chassis, minimum. This man Ron was an ex marine engineer; where there was a little space on the walls, it was taken up with pictures of ancient ships. Doubtless he would have had those real ships disassembled and in his house if he could, and as Erik set about collecting his MG parts harvest he could see the pain he was causing Ron.

The old boy did not want to part with a single washer, and here was a supermarket of MG entrails that would have sent any dealer into a slavering fit of avarice. Erik, taking pity, confined himself to a modest hoard, and paid.

Erik and Pam Benson are currently running a 1951 TD in fading Clipper Blue. It does look rather nice where they live, does it not? All that sunshine. Different to Glasgow.

ers.

Here is Pam giving Erik a good-luck kiss before the race at Les Remparts, Angoulême, in the 1939 TB, like the ones owned by three brothers from a rather grand family in Perthshire. They were bought for the boys to come back to, after the war, but first one was killed, then the next, then the next, so the cars were covered over. They stayed that way until mother died, when they were shipped to Australia.

In 1992, Erik had the idea of entering a team of three T racers at the Circuit des Remparts, Angoulême in SW France. It's ideal for Ts, blasting through narrow stone walled streets and weaving round tight hairpins in the sun. Freddie Yhap, Glyn Giusti and Erik had respectively a TA, TB and TD, and their name was Team Rosbif. Coincidentally, the cars were all metallic silver with wings in their own colours. Their exploits are now known all over France and they have their own cup, Le Plat du Jour, for the most impressive performance of the event.

Erik (in foreground) rebuilt his 1939 TB Special from chassis up. Known privately as The Giant Killer, it was so powerful and fast that it could beat the GP Bugatti drivers into a cocked hat and even get among the ERAs, much to their discomposition.

CHAPTER THIRTY ONE

Klubben För Alla Som Är Intresserade Av MG

Most little boys are interested in sport and cars. In Sweden, the young Berndt Aulin was interested in sports cars, and devoured every magazine and every piece of information he could find on the subject. By age eleven he had settled on three favourites: MG, Jaguar and Aston Martin (no Volvo or Saab, apparently), although he had yet to see any of them in the flesh, as it were.

One Sunday morning in 1957, he went out of the house to find a miracle. All along his street stood a row of sports cars, mostly MGs and mostly T-types. The ones he recognised were TCs; he hadn't really heard about the others and didn't understand the differences, though they were probably there, but all he wanted to do was walk up and down and wonder. Friends accompanied him for a while but they'd soon seen enough, while for Berndt there was no such thing as enough.

At last, the cars were started and driven away, leaving a bewitched boy with a head full of big wheels, long bonnets, slab tanks, radiators almost behind front axles, sounds, colours, chrome and unalloyed excitement. His determination to have a TC – for that model had now supplanted all other possibilities – only increased with the years.

He finished school, worked for a while, went up to the University of Lund to read economics, found a lovely girlfriend he intended to marry, and saw an ad in the paper. Classic sports car MG TC for sale. No price was mentioned but Berndt was sure it would be beyond the reach of an impoverished student. This opinion he declaimed at large and in strong language to anyone who would listen, which was his girlfriend. If confirmation were needed of Eva's magnificent qualities, it came with her offer of all her worldly goods, 5,000 kronor (about £350 at the time).

The seller said the car was in good order, having been restored by the previous owner, and could be had for the bargain price of 14,500 kronor, or three times Berndt's best offer. He assuaged his disappointment by buying a model of the TC and a workshop manual. If he couldn't have one yet, he would educate himself in the meantime.

Berndt married his girl, joined the Automobilhistoriska Klubben and set about improving the financial position of the Aulins. By 1980 he was well enough situated to answer positively when the call came, saying that there was a TC some miles away, lying in a pile on a garage floor. The owner wouldn't sell, not even after several months of nagging phone calls, but he did admit in the end that he might sell his TB.

Berndt Aulin wanted a TC but ended up buying a heap of junk that was mostly TB but partly TA. What with one thing and another, it would take fourteen years from the junk to the top down, summer's day, country lane experience that was the dream, and an awful lot of work in between.

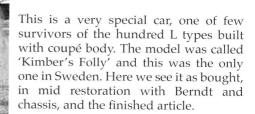

This is a very special car, one of few survivors of the hundred L types built with coupé body. The model was called 'Kimber's Folly' and this was the only one in Sweden. Here we see it as bought, in mid restoration with Berndt and chassis, and the finished article.

Thinking that a switch sale might be possible, Berndt took the train to the other side of Sweden, was picked up in a Morgan and given the driver's seat. The Morgan was a new experience but it didn't change his mind. He still wanted a TC. Somehow, the heap of junk he was shown did change his mind, and now he was overcome with the urge to rebuild the rarer TB, a pre-war model, a car made in 1939 when the founding father Cecil Kimber was still in charge, and the rarest of the T-types, only 379 built from May 1939 until the switch to war work.

Next weekend, a friend took his father's car and a trailer and drove about 400 km to pick up the car. Everything went swimmingly until they got back to Berndt's house and Eva saw the sad heap of junk about which he had waxed so lyrical. Her opinion was that the erstwhile owner should have paid Berndt to take such rubbish away. She was backed by the laughing neighbours but, bearing in mind that they all laughed at Christopher Columbus, when he said the world was round, and they all laughed when Edison recorded sound, Berndt closed the garage door and began.

He soon found that the radiator and steering column came from a TA. Another customer of this same dealer called to say that the pile of junk he'd bought as a TA contained a radiator and steering column from a TB. They swapped and have been friends ever since. If only the rest had been so easy, but it wasn't. Berndt realised that he couldn't finish any phase of the restoration, however small, because parts were always missing or defunct. He became a regular customer of NTG Motors of Ipswich, and gave an immediate yes to an invitation from friends to go to the Beaulieu Autojumble. One friend was especially expert on T-series parts and got Berndt to buy bits and pieces he had no idea he needed. Heading back for the ferry they called in at NTG with a long list, and boarded the ship feeling they ought to park centrally or they might tip the whole vessel over. Another worry was the customs at Helsingborg, who might not recognise MG parts for the harmless technology they represented, but they didn't look.

Berndt's garage now looked like a spare parts shop. Everything was on the shelves, like a well stocked supermarket, and the rebuild went on apace. Even so, when he finished and had the car registered and tested, he had to be reminded that he'd been on the job for fourteen years.

So what? Driving it was even better than he had thought. Sun, rain, wind, who cared? Two weeks after the first drive, Berndt and Eva drove 350 km to a big, all-Scandinavia MG meeting that lasted three days including rally, dinner and dance, *Concours d'Élégance* and so on. They won the *Concours* in their class and the following year an Outstanding Renovation Award, the prize for which was a model MG radiator, hollow, in sterling silver, with the names of all the winners engraved on the reverse. At the end of his holding year, the most recent winner had to return the radiator filled with whisky.

The long Swedish winter began and, for the first time in fourteen years, Berndt had nothing to do on those dark, dark nights. He built a boat the first winter but that didn't really do much for him, then the chap with whom he'd swapped radiators and steering column all that time before, rang him and said he had a part-restored L1 Magna Continental Coupé from 1933. He was too busy with other things to finish it. Eva persuaded a reluctant Berndt to buy it.

The car was almost complete, no heap of junk, with the body's ash-frame done, and seats and panels upholstered in dark green leather. It seemed to cry out, 'Restore me'. What could Berndt do but agree? The model was named 'Kimber's Folly' because it so missed the taste of the age and was a very slow seller, while the two-seater version of the L-type was much more popular. Still, Berndt was fascinated with its odd lines, bucket seats, leather and pockets everywhere, arm rests, circular ash trays – all the luxuries of pre-war gracious living.

To start with, the disassembly and sandblasting, hours and hours of it, instilled feelings of desperation but after some months he had a rolling chassis that looked like new. The engine was untouched so far and he wondered if he should do the work on it himself. It looked more complicated than the XPAG engine for the TB. A friend offered to sort the cylinder head, which he did, and later the rest of the engine but that turned out not to need any work. Friend thought that the engine must have been rebuilt just before the car was taken off the road 60 years before. They put it back in the chassis, connected everything, and she started immediately. They listened, enraptured, to a six cylinder OHC MG engine that had been at rest for more than half a century. Magical music.

With more work the chassis was drivable and became a short-term exhibit at the newly opened car museum, Autoseum, in Simrishamn. Before leaving it there, Berndt drove the chassis ten times round the building, 'my mind filled with joy'.

Some of the body's aluminium panels needed repair and some had to be replaced. Berndt got an expert on the job but he came to a stop at the sliding roof. Nobody knew how the roof was supposed to look. Berndt contacted other owners – Martin Barett in Australia, Max Nosbuch in Luxembourg, Paul Leers in Holland, Wiard Krook in Belgium, but none of them knew all the answers.

Terry Andrews in the UK found a car that had been standing outside under a cover for sixty five years, complete except for the clock and, naturally, the sliding roof. Terry took information from all the others and, with his friend James Petitte, worked it out. They met in Holland in November 2009. Terry explained what he and James had done and offered to order roofs for all their cars.

So, in March 2010, the members of the L Continental Coupé Group met in Belgium at the European Workshop organised by Stefaan Vernyns. Terry delivered new sliding roofs, complete with tracks and fittings.

When he first bought his pile of MG junk, Berndt joined MGCC Sweden, which was the best car thing he ever did. 'I have many good friends who always want to give a helping hand. There is always somebody who has heard about a missing part or knows somebody who can fix a problem you can't manage yourself, and the same can be said about all MG people.' Which, Berndt, seems like a good message to finish on.

I said MGB, not MB

But first, what does Wartburg mean to you? To some it means the castle where Martin Luther did his Latin-to-German translation of the New Testament. To something less than a thousand of the good citizens of Tennessee, it is their home town, and to rather more than that it's a Lutheran (see above) seminary in Iowa. To a few pitiable individuals, it's the name of the first sports car BMW made. To most of us, however, it's the name of the firm supplying the latest must-haves in infant care, including the truly remarkable 'Bumbo' baby seat.

And there's the other car, of course, or we wouldn't be mentioning it, powered by a three cylinder two-stroke engine with seven moving parts, requiring a service every 30,000 miles. This makes it a considerably more complex vehicle than the equally brilliant East German Trabant, the engine of which has only five moving parts.

To conclude our brief diversion behind the Iron Curtain, we must take a peek at the Škoda 1000 MB, the very first rear engined Škoda model in mass production. The name MB came from the first letters of the manufacturing city, Mladà Boleslav, now in the Czech Republic, then Czechoslovakia. The car was not exactly up with the times when it came out, although space-age compared with its predecessor, the Octavia.

The engine was interesting, with an aluminium alloy block and a cast-iron head. Lubrication of the main bearings was intermittent, oil pressure was low and the engine was prone to overheating. The heater was a novelty, having been placed under the back seat for increased driver comfort. So, an MGB it is, then.

Reports of the death of the MGC are premature
Extract from article in *Autocar* magazine, December 1970:

It is hard to say exactly what killed the MGC, but the most likely cause was the bad press the car received, together with its failure to sell in the USA. Our own road test, published in 16 November 1967, was far from enthusiastic about the engine, gearbox, handling and fuel consumption. Exactly when production ceased is hard to determine, but it was sometime last year. University Motors bought the last batch of cars and have been selling them successfully since. Their theory was that, with only a little attention, the model could be improved significantly and as they still have some 20 or so cars in stock, we decided to test one to find out for ourselves.

Basically they are offering an MGC GT in standard paint, with wire wheels, delivered with number plates, seat belts and four months tax for £1,370. At the Motor Show in 1968, the listed price was £1,337 without any of these extras, or even a heater. By today's standards this is about £130 less than a Triumph TR6 coupé and not very much more than a GT6 delivered to the same specification. To improve the appeal though, they are also offering a long list of extras, most of these being fitted to the test car. Added together these came to another £460, making the test car £1,830, or about as much as an Alfa Romeo 1300 GT or a little more than a BMW 2002. Some of these make so much difference as to be near essentials, while others like the stereo tape player and radio (£92) are pretty obvious luxuries.

Items like the Downton engine conversion make such a difference as to qualify as essential extras and the overall effect on the car leaves one wondering why it could not have been made like this in the first place, and if it had, would the fate of the model have been more successful? It would certainly have been much more enthusiastically received by our staff.

As a single item the Downton kit costs £175 fitted. It comprises the usual kind of head improvement, coupled with special manifolds and a complete transformation of the induction system. In standard form the MGC is a real pig when cold, developing hardly any power until warm and never idling reliably. The Downton-converted car suffers from none of these troubles, pulling eagerly straight after a cold start. More than just this, the conversion gives the engine the 'right' kind of sporty response, which it never displayed in standard form, climbing on to the cam at about 3,000rpm with a real bark to its straight-through exhaust. In many ways it reminds one of the works rally Healey 3000, both in overall response and the noise it makes.

Actual improvements in acceleration time are not spectacular, but very worthwhile none the less. In top, for example, about 2 seconds is knocked off each 20mph increment. Standing start times show similar slight improvements, and we could probably have made the differences greater if we had not been fooled by the rev counter, which over-read by almost 500 rpm at the top end.

As well as improving the performance, the conversion works wonders for the over-all fuel consumption. Driving the car hard we got very nearly 20mpg, which compares with only 17.5mpg for the standard product.

The standard gearbox, with its enigmatic choice of ratios, remains unchanged, as does the final drive ratio with its long-legged 26.95 mph per 1,000rpm in overdrive top. The test car was fitted with Cosmic light alloy wheels (£60 for five) which did little for the roadholding, but improved the appearance no end. They were fitted with the standard Dunlop radial-ply tyres.

Another worthwhile improvement came from the substitution of Koni dampers (£16 the pair, fitted) at the front and a 15 inch diameter Motolita leather-trimmed steering wheel (£12 12s). Standard wheel size was 16.5in, so the steering becomes that much more responsive and the view out ahead that much better. Wooden packing strips under the seat runners also improved the driving position, which on the standard car was far too low for anyone much under 6ft tall.

Giving less leverage, the smaller wheel increases the already heavy steering effort, making fast cornering quite a muscular struggle. Excessive understeer from the extra nose weight of the six-cylinder engine makes the MGC a much less lithesome car than the MGB, but it is impressively stable in a straight line as compensation. Poor turning circles (almost 36ft between kerbs) hamper one when manoeuvring.

It would be wrong for a true sports car enthusiast to look at the MGC and expect it to be one better than the MGB. In the vital qualities of handling and engine response, it is no match for the four-cylinder car. But as a long-distance touring car, where a lot of the distance covered will be on motorways, it definitely has a place and in University Motors' guise begins to look much more attractive. At £1,545 (£1,370 plus the essential Downton conversion) it has few direct competitors, and anyone worried about spending this much on an obsolete model can take comfort in the fact that its rarity alone may one day make it a sought-after classic. According to factory records, only 2,199 MGC GTs have been delivered in the UK.

Epilogue for a car man

'Right you are!' cried the Rat, starting up. 'We'll rescue the poor unhappy animal! We'll convert him! He'll be the most converted Toad that ever was before we're done with him!'

They set off up the road on their mission of mercy, Badger leading the way…(they) reached the carriage-drive of Toad Hall to find, as the Badger had anticipated, a shiny new motor car, of great size, painted a bright red (Toad's favourite colour), standing in front of the house. As they neared the door it was flung open, and Mr. Toad, arrayed in goggles, cap, gaiters, and enormous overcoat, came swaggering down the steps, drawing on his gauntleted gloves…The Badger strode up the steps. 'Take him inside,' he said sternly to his companions…

…'My friends,' the Badger went on, 'I am pleased to inform you that Toad has at last seen the error of his ways. He is truly sorry for his misguided conduct in the past, and he has undertaken to give up motor-cars entirely and for ever. I have his solemn promise to that effect.'

'That is very good news,' said the Mole gravely.

'Very good news indeed,' observed the Rat dubiously, 'if only – if only –'

The Wind in the Willows, Kenneth Grahame.

NUOVA–3 LITRI MGC. SICURA E VELOCE. BELLA
VETTURA SPORTIVA INGLESE. CONVERTIBILE O
GT. TRASMISSIONE MANUALE O AUTOMATICA
L.1,715,966

Parliamo Inglese

3-litri MGC	3-litre MGC
Sicura e veloce	safety fast
Bella vettura sportiva inglese	beautiful English sports car
Manuale o automatica	automatic or manual transmission
L.1,715,966	£1145.13.1 1 (inc. £250.13.11 PT)

The British Motor Corporation Ltd,
Longbridge, Birmingham

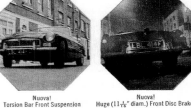

Nuova!
Torsion Bar Front Suspension

Nuova!
Huge ($11\frac{1}{8}$" diam.) Front Disc Brakes

Nuova! MGC/GT
£1299.0.7 (inc. £284.0.7 PT)

In 1968 in Italy, you could have had a C for 1,716,000 lire, give or take a lira or two, or £1,145 if you paid in sterling (£1,300 for the GT). *Sicura e veloce, manuale o automatico,* we can only wonder what happened to LBL 414F, the car that appears in this ad simultaneously in blue and red.

Why MG? A man called Bill rebuilt a pair of 1939 TBs and made a brilliant job of them, without any outside help. Having worn earphones at work for many years, he fell to cancer in the glands behind his ears. The operation and treatment worked, but one side of his face slipped and disfigured him. He could get rather miserable a lot of the time and needed cheering up, so his pal Erik Benson suggested that he take one of the MGs, fill the tank, put the hood and the windscreen down, drive until the fuel was gone, refill and do it again until all cobwebs were mere atoms of memory. Bill did as he was told. The little car made him smile again, and he never was miserable thereafter. Of course, it doesn't have to be a TB. It could be a TD, like this one of Bob McCluskey's, and it needn't be Australia. Bill lived in Warwickshire. But the point remains.

What can we say? What can be said? MG – where beauty comes as standard.

Appendix

MG marques

- 1924–1926; Morris Bullnose 14/28
- 1926–1927; Morris Flatnose 14/28
- 1927–1929; MG 14/40
- 1928–1931; 18/80 Mark I
- 1929–1932; M-type Midget
- 1930–1933; 18/80 Mark II
- 1930–1931; 18/100 (18 Mark III later known as Tigress)
- 1931–1932; C-type Midget
- 1931–1932; D-type Midget
- 1931–1932; F-type Magna
- 1932–1934; J-type Midget
- 1932–1934; K-type Magnette
- 1933–1934; L-type Magna
- 1933–1934; KN
- 1934; Q-type
- 1934–1936; N-type Magnette
- 1935; R-type
- 1934–1936; P-type Midget

- 1936–1939; TA Midget
- 1936–1939; SA
- 1937–1939; VA
- 1938–1939; WA
- 1939–1940; TB Midget
- 1945–1950; TC Midget
- 1947–1953; Y-type
- 1950–1953; TD Midget
- 1953–1955; TF Midget
- 1953–1956; Magnette ZA
- 1955–1962; MGA
- 1956–1958; Magnette ZB
- 1959–1961; Magnette Mark III
- 1961–1968; Magnette Mark IV
- 1961–1979; MG Midget
- 1962–1980; MGB
- 1968–1969; MGC
- 1973–1976; MGB GT V8

Two Ts on Carlton Bank, a typical piece of the North Yorkshire Moors where the hills are steep and the sheep are man-eaters.

Acknowledgements

Photograph of police TC courtesy of Kent Police Museum, The Historic Dockyard, Chatham ME4 4TE, www.kent-police-museum.co.uk. Classic MG advertisements courtesy of Hermann Egges; see www.car-brochures.eu. Stamps courtesy of Willem van der Veer; see www.mgstamps.shorturl.com.

Falling in love again, never wanted to. What am I to do? I can't help it.

The open road, somewhere in France on a fine early morning, a good lunch in prospect, and my TB bowling happily along. There cannot be many things in this world better than that.

This 1950 TD featured in the book *Car Driving as an Art* by S C H 'Sammy' Davis. It looks even better now, on a sunny day in the Goyt Valley, near Buxton, Derbyshire.

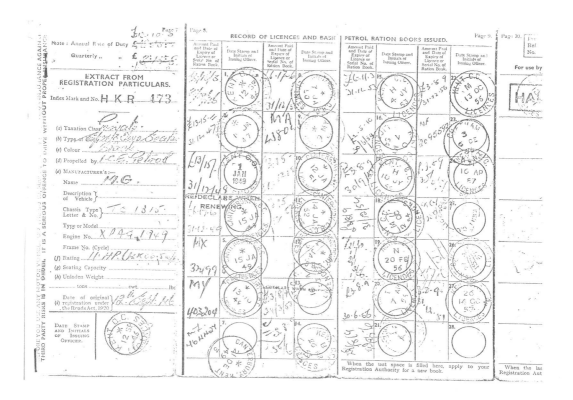

HKR 473 was a British police car in 1946/47. Now she's restored in Nova Scotia.

Cars? Just heaps of tin. Go from A to B to C.